Guide To
Lake and Stream
Trout Fishing

BILL HERZOG

Frank
Amato
PORTLAND

Dedication

To Brenda, who keeps my spirits high and makes me go fishing.

Acknowledgments

The following men, past and present, gave much time, support and information for this book: to "The Wizard of American Lake", Uncle Bob Pollen, who taught me how to catch more kokanee than I could carry; to Mark Renner, with whom I spent my youthful summers hiking hundreds of miles of cutthroat streams; Uncle Jack Thompson, who showed me how to troll and find trout in lakes, and finally to Dave Hughes for his observations on trout foods and behavior.

About the Author

Jed Davis Photo

Bill Herzog currently lives near Seattle, Washington, where he has fished for trout, salmon and steelhead most of his 35 years. When Bill isn't fishing or bowling he is working as a writer and is in charge of Special Projects for Amato Publications. Bill is also the author of *Spoon fishing for Steelhead, Color Guide to Steelhead Drift Fishing, Beginner's Guide to Bass Fishing* and is a regular contributor to *Salmon Trout Steelheader* magazine.

Protection of Wild Trout

We encourage you to crimp down the barbs on your hooks and release wild trout. When using bait, set the hook quickly so that the trout does not take it deep into its throat. Hatchery trout can be taken to eat because they are replaced by the state. For good sport for all, however, please limit your kill! Catch and release is the future if we want to enjoy good fishing!

© 1994 Frank Amato Publications Inc.

All rights reserved. No part of this book may be reproduced in any way without the express written consent of the publisher, except in the case of brief excerpts in critical reviews and articles. All inquiries should be addressed to:

Frank Amato Publications Inc.
PO Box 82112
Portland, Oregon 97282
(503) 653-8108

Photo Credits:

Bill Herzog—4, 7 left, 9 left, 17, 20, 21, 22, 27, 28 top, 29, 42
Jim Schollmeyer—11, 12, 13, 24, 26, 32, 33, 34, 35, 36, 37, 38, 39, 40, 41, 45
Frank Amato—6, 8, 10, 14, 15, 18, 19, 23, 25, 28 bottom, 43, 46
Jim Bedford—7 right
Jed Davis—9 right, 31
Bill Stinson—44
Front and Back Cover Photographs: Bill Herzog

Book design and layout: Tony Amato

Softbound ISBN: 1-878175-82-3
UPC: 0-66066-00166-5

Printed in HONG KONG

10 9 8 7 6 5 4 3 2

CONTENTS

Introduction

I am one of the fortunate few who associates sportfishing with occupation. During the winter of 1992-93, most of my time was spent on the International Sportsman's Exhibition circuit along the West Coast. During this time I had the pleasure of talking to literally hundreds of fishermen from all walks of life. Some were steelheaders, some bass fishermen, others spent their most enjoyable hours pursuing salmon. However, nearly half were lake and stream trout fishermen—not fly fishermen, mind you, but traditional gear fishers with bait and lures. Many inquiries were for a basic non-fly fishing "how to" book for lake and stream trout. We feel *Guide to Lake and Stream Trout Fishing* fills that void.

Unquestionably, trout fishing is one of the most popular piscatorial pursuits in America. Virtually every state supports populations of trout, even some warmer southern states and Hawaii have trout. The environs where trout are found are diverse—from treeless high elevation lakes to lowland ponds, from crashing mountain brooks to slow meandering meadow streams and from mammoth rivers, to lakes and reservoirs.

Rarely will you meet an angler on a lake or stream who did not start out as a youngster with a can of worms, jar of salmon eggs or tiny twinkling spinner. We start with these methods because they produce, sometimes so well in fact that they can overcome inexperience. One constant that does remain from our early trout encounters is the satisfaction derived from using these techniques. As adults we choose to stay with them because they produce. *Guide to Lake and Stream Trout Fishing* will take time-honored traditional techniques a step further and make them more effective.

This book covers the basics, also touching on topics not found in most "how to" manuals. Information is geared to help increase your hookups while on lake or stream. Chapter One introduces and discusses the trout. You will notice that some species were omitted from the list. Not without good reason, however. The trout mentioned are the most common, have the largest range and are readily available to the general public. Golden trout, lake trout and Arctic char, for example, were left out due to their relatively small range, difficulty of access and specialized angling techniques. Nowhere in the book will you see a photo of a dead trout. Though there are many put-and-take fisheries, the future of fishing dictates that fishermen adopt a catch and release ethic toward wild fish (and in certain cases hatchery-origin fish) to ensure quality fishing into the future.

Chapter Two covers natural trout foods. To fool and hook trout, it helps greatly to know what they eat, as trout behavior revolves around finding food. Knowing what trout eat, seasonally and geographically, allows you to "match the hatch," so to speak when choosing a bait or lure.

Chapter Three is the most important part of the book—how to find trout in lakes and streams. You will see how to recognize and identify holding areas in rivers, streams and creeks, as well as learn how to locate trout in stillwater fisheries of lakes and reservoirs. Trout fishing is a year-round pursuit, not just a summertime activity. This chapter demonstrates how to find trout in lakes and streams during any month of the year. Once you learn how to locate trout, half the battle is won.

Chapter Four teaches you which outfits properly match your chosen method of trout fishing. We will cover rods, reels and lines to make your fishing more effective and pleasant.

Chapter Five explains the most popular and effective techniques for taking trout: trolling and stillfishing lakes, and how to present lures and bait in rivers and creeks. I also cover the "fly and bubble" technique that borrows from two different methods: spin casting and fly fishing. Lastly, we will see how to properly handle and release trout.

Enjoy and learn from *Guide to Lake and Stream Trout Fishing*. Twenty million trout anglers from coast to coast can't be wrong.

Chapter 1

American Trout, Char and Landlocked Salmon

No other gamefish in America has had as many books and articles written about it as the trout. However popular bass and walleye may be, trout have a 400 year lead on both in angling literature. There are close to 100 different species and sub-species of trout that have captured the imaginations of North American writers, but there are six in particular that are most commonly found by Lower 48 anglers. These six, which include true trouts (rainbow, brown and cutthroat), char (brook and Dolly Varden) and kokanee salmon will be discussed here.

We will look at each trout individually, giving a brief but detailed description of distribution and range, identification by markings and coloration, feeding habits and temperature range. This chapter will help you understand each species and its availability.

True Trouts

Rainbow *(Oncorhynchus mykiss)*

The rainbow is native to lakes and rivers that empty into the Pacific Ocean. It is found in Russia, Alaska, British Columbia, Washington, Oregon, California and portions of Mexico. Wherever rainbows have access to saltwater, they spend one to five years feeding and growing before returning to freshwater to spawn. An adaptable trout, it has been planted across the United States, Canada, Africa, New Zealand, the British Isles and South America. Thanks to hatcheries we now have rainbows in every state that can support trout. Legendary for its acrobatic abilities, with numerous leaps its trademark, the rainbow is considered by many to be the best fighter of all trouts.

Rainbows are recognized by pink/magenta coloration on the gillplates and a pinkish-red stripe down the lateral line. Rainbows from large lakes, or sea-run (steelhead) are dark gun-metal blue/black along the back, with silver sides that melt into a bright white belly. There is little evidence of the color/stripe on fresh sea-run fish or lake fish during the non-spawning season. During spawning season (late winter to early spring) colors are more vivid. Rainbows have black spots, varying from a few dots along the back to heavily spotted over the entire body. Males are decidedly more colorful than females.

The rainbow is a trout of fast flowing water preferring to lay in riffles, on current edges in fast water and behind obstructions such as boulders. They use these lies not only for protection from predators, but also as feeding stations. Not a particularly fussy eater the rainbow will take almost

any available food. Stream rainbows eat primarily aquatic and terrestrial insects, however, they are opportunistic feeders eating salmon and trout spawn (eggs), salmon fry and even flesh from decaying salmon during the fall season. Larger lake fish target smaller fish as their main diet, along with insects. Sea-going rainbow eat primarily squid and shrimp. Rainbow prefer a water temperature range of 45 to 58 degrees, with a maximum tolerance of 70 degrees. These temperatures are keys to finding them when probing the depths of lakes and impoundments.

Rainbows vary in size according to habitat. A large specimen from a high mountain stream may be 10 inches while rainbow from food-rich large inland lakes may easily go over 20 pounds. Steelhead have been documented to 42 pounds, but the average sea-run rainbow will be between 5 and 12 pounds. Rainbows from some British Columbia lakes have been documented to over 50 pounds, however, most rainbows will be one-half to 2 pounds.

Cutthroat *(Oncorhynchus clarki)*

The cutthroat is native to the western United States and Canada from southwest Alaska to Mexico. It is found in all states west of the Rocky Mountains. The cutthroat is not as hardy a fish as the rainbow and has not responded well to plants outside its range. When cutthroat have access to saltwater they will travel there to feed, staying close to parent streams. This migrant, the sea-run or coastal cutthroat, is one of several important sub-species of cutthroat readily available to the angler. Along with the coastal variety is the Yellowstone, Lahontan and Montana black spot. Rated as one of the easiest trout to catch, it readily attacks lures and baits. The cutthroat fights hard for its size, jumping occasionally and staying underwater for most of the battle.

Cutthroat closely resemble rainbow in many waters, partially due to the cutthroat's tendency to cross-breed with rainbow. However true cutthroats always carry their namesake, a slash of color under each gill cover that varies from light yellow to dark, fire red. Males and cutthroats in spawning stage have more vividly colored slashes. Body colors vary from pale green to blue-green backs and silver sides on sea-run fish, to olive green or brown backs with yellow-silver sides on resident cutthroat. Resident stream and lake cutthroats have reddish-pink gill covers and white-tipped fins. Cutthroat are late fall/early winter spawners, and their colors are pronounced during this time. All cutthroat have black spots which vary greatly. Coastal cuts, for example, may have tiny black spots covering their entire bodies, while a Montana black spot might have a few large spots near and on the tail. One sure way to distinguish cutthroat from rainbow is to check for teeth on the back of the tongue. Cutthroat have them, rainbows do not.

Stream cutthroat shy away from water types that traditionally hold rainbow, preferring to lie in current edges and slower water. Stream cuts are also "hiders," that is they can be typically found under cut banks, submerged logs, sweeper tree branches and other structures. Cutthroat are coldwater trout, preferring lake and stream temperatures ranging from 38 to 54 degrees, with a tolerance to 65 degrees. They feed primarily on aquatic insects, nymphs in particular, and also terrestrials. Lake-bound cutthroat also target smaller fish, especially once they reach several pounds. Sea-run cutthroat eat sculpin, krill (tiny shrimp) and small bait fish.

Cutthroat vary in size, depending on environment and food supply. Sea-run or coastal stream cutthroat range from 6 to 20 inches, while lake varieties of other species range from 14 inches to 6 pounds. The Lahontan species grows largest, and is more tolerable of adverse conditions than other cutthroats. The world record cutthroat is a 41-pound Lahontan from Nevada's Pyramid Lake in 1925. Unfortunately, this sub-species of giants was officially declared extinct in 1938.

Brown *(Salmo trutta)*

The brown trout is perhaps the most important, and successfully adapted, species of gamefish imported into North America. Michigan's upper Pere Marquette River saw the first plantings of German browns in 1883. More tolerant of warmer, siltier water than other trout species, the brown was a welcome substitute for brook trout and grayling that disappeared from eastern waters after deforestation destroyed their habitat. Browns thrive in lakes and streams where there would not be any opportunity for trout fishing otherwise. Native to Europe, Asia and the British Isles, browns have also been successfully transplanted to New Zealand, Africa and South America. When browns have access to saltwater, they will migrate to feed and upon returning to their home stream sport bright silver flanks. In northern Europe, Chile and Argentina, sea-run browns are the primary sport fish. Browns are considered to be the most difficult of all trouts to catch, and when hooked fight a hard, underwater battle, leaping occasionally.

Since different strains of brown trout have been cross-bred (in the wild as well as in hatcheries) combining German, Asian and Scottish strains, their identification varies with the areas in which they are found. Typically they will be anywhere from black/dark brown on the back, with sides varying from yellow to almost silver. Browns have dark brown, black and red spots on their sides. During their fall spawning season, browns develop a reddish hue on their fins and belly. Not needing as much oxygen as rainbows, browns are found in most any type of holding water, from riffles to current edges to deep, slow pools, with a preference for moderate currents. Brown do best at a temperature of approximately 60 degrees, but thrive well in lakes and streams that vary between 52 and 70 degrees. Primarily an aquatic insect eater, browns are opportunistic feeders that eat anything that happens along, including mice and snakes. Large browns are nocturnal feeders, and it is during night-time hours that some of the biggest fish are caught. Browns have a cannibalistic streak, they will eat smaller browns. Brown trout four pounds and larger are fond of crayfish and tiny fish such as sculpin, minnows and suckers.

Due to their longevity and diet, the brown is one of the largest trouts. Sea-run varieties can average 10 pounds; stream browns will typically be 12 inches to 5 pounds, while lake and impoundment fish can reach the 30-pound mark.

Chars

Brook *(Salvelinus fontinalis)*

The brook trout is native to eastern North America from the Appalachian Mountains to the Hudson Bay drainage in Labrador and Quebec. A trout of cold water, it has been successfully planted west of the Rocky Mountains in clear, pure

high elevation lakes and streams and many lowland waters that stay cold and clean enough to support brook trout populations. The "brookie" has anadromous tendencies, some species will go to sea. These sea-run brook trout are called "coasters." Brook trout are seldom hard to catch. Due to their voracious appetite they are regarded as the easiest

trout to hook. Brooks rarely get airborne, they fight a dogged, underwater battle characterized by open-mouth head shakes.

There is little argument that the brook trout is the most colorful of common trouts. Identification is easy, as brookies look the same regardless of the area they are found. Brook trout have "worm" markings on olive-green backs, called vermiculations. Their sides are silvery, bellies are orange and have red spots inside rings of brilliant blue. Fins are reddish with black and white edges. All these colors are more vivid when they spawn in late fall. Sea-run brooks are primarily silver on the sides with faint markings that characterize brook trout. Brooks prefer riffles and highly oxygenated water, but can also be found hiding beneath submerged logs, overhanging tree branches and undercut banks. Brook trout prefer a temperature range of 38 to 60 degrees, with an optimum temperature of 55 degrees. They feed almost exclusively on aquatic insects and small fishes, sculpin in particular, but also eat terrestrials when available.

Three factors determine brook trout size: angling pressure, availability of food and longevity. Because they are so easy to catch, most brooks are caught before they attain double-digit length in inches. A full grown brook trout from a high mountain lake or stream may only be 8 inches long, due to lack of food and overpopulation. In northeastern Canada there are fewer brook trout, waters are richer, streams are larger and fish live longer. Large 2 to 8 pound brookies, affectionately called "squaretails," are not uncommon in this area. Another area recently discovered for trophy brookies is on the British Columbia/Alberta border in Hamber Provincial park. Brook trout in northern streams and lakes live for many years and it takes perhaps a decade to grow a large trout of 6 pounds. The world record brook trout of 11 pounds came from the Nipigon River. Most brook trout caught in the States will be 6 to 12 inches long.

Dolly Varden and Bull Trout *(Salvelinus malma)*

The Dolly is native to the Pacific drainage from Oregon up through western Alaska and inland to western Montana. Dolly Varden and bull trout look identical; the difference between them is Dollies have access to saltwater, but bull trout are primarily landlocked. You may find bull trout in

Landlocked Salmon

Kokanee (Sockeye) *(Oncorhynchus nerka)*

The kokanee, a landlocked sockeye salmon, is managed as a trout by game departments and is a highly prized game fish. Kokanee live primarily in western lakes and impoundments, but excellent fisheries are available in larger rivers. Kokanee are found in northern California, Oregon, Washington, southern British Columbia, Idaho, western Montana, Wyoming and Colorado. They have been successfully planted in the Great Lakes and other eastern states. When caught on ultra-light gear, kokanee put up a tremendous fight and commonly leap several times when they feel the hook. They have deep red flesh and are regarded as the best eating "trout." Primarily plankton eaters, kokanee take a variety of baits and trolled lures.

Kokanee are silvery and pleasing to the eye. A kokanee has no spots and a forked tail, two traits that visually separate them from trout. Deep-blue backs with silver sides and a bright white belly characterize this fish during winter, spring and summer. During autumn, the kokanee's spawning season, mature fish turn bright red over the entire body and fins, with a forest green head. Kokanee are schooling fish, where you find one you are bound to find dozens more. In lakes and impoundments they inhabit depths with temperatures of 46 to 60 degrees, with a favorite of 55 degrees. These temperatures are a rough guideline to finding kokanee. Depending mostly on degree of lighting and surface disturbance, kokanee can be found a few feet to 80 feet down.

Montana, Idaho, Washington, British Columbia and parts of Alaska, while Dolly Varden are found primarily on the coastal strip of North America, and Korea and Russia. The Dolly has not been planted outside its range. It is found in cold waters, usually of glacial origin. Sea-run Dolly Varden are common from northern Washington to Alaska, returning silver and well-proportioned. An aggressive biter, Dollies are fairly easy to catch and put up a decent underwater fight. Because of aggressive tendencies, the Dolly attacks spoons, spinners or bait with gusto.

Like its close relative the brook trout, the Dolly lacks black spots and is relatively simple to identify. Landlocked bull trout have dark green backs and dull silver sides with primarily yellow and occasionally light pink spots. Dollies also have faint vermiculations on the back along with yellow spots and red spots on or below the lateral line. Both Dollies and bull trout have grey fins sporting white and black edges. Dollies are fall spawners and during this time often display a touch of red on the belly. Sea-run dollies have dark olive backs, chrome-silver sides and faint yellow and pink spots. Dolly Varden and bull trout are cold water species that prefer a range of 34 to 55 degrees, the optimum temperature being 45 degrees. They seek deep holes in rivers, but can also be found in riffles and current edges waiting to ambush small fish. Dollies and bull trout are opportunistic feeders, they eat almost anything small enough to fit in their mouths. Their primary foods are sculpin, small fish (like baby salmon) and salmon eggs in season. Because this diet includes salmon smolts the Dolly has long endured a bad reputation.

If you believe fish tales, an old fishing companion used live white mice to coax bull trout up to 20 pounds from deep holes in the glacial streams that flow from Mount Rainier!

Dollies live many years, but due to cold water conditions are slow growers. A 20-inch bull trout from a sterile glacial stream may be a year old for every inch it is long. Sea-run varieties run between 16 inches and 10 pounds, while lake-bound and large river strains attain weights close to 30 pounds. The world-record lake Dolly Varden is 32 pounds taken from Lake Pend Orelle in Idaho; the record sea-run Dolly is 10 pounds from western Washington's Skykomish River. Most Dollies and bull trout are between 12 inches and 4 pounds.

Due to a tendency to overpopulate, most kokanee are small, 7 to 10 inches long and weigh less than a pound. For this reason, many bodies of water where kokanee are found include a bonus limit to help keep populations down. Lakes with smaller kokanee populations provide opportunities for larger fish averaging 14 to 18 inches and up to 2-1/2 pounds. The record kokanee is approximately 4 pounds.

Chapter 2

Trout Foods

Lakes and streams contain a wide variety of organisms that trout target as food sources. Each body of water varies in food source and knowing which foods are dominant in the river or lake you plan to fish will help you find and catch trout. Trout are opportunistic feeders, eating whatever is palatable or available. Steelhead, large resident rainbows, browns and Dolly Varden seem to illustrate this point best, as stomach contents of a few fish have contained rocks, ball-point pen caps, lemmings (mice), snakes and small water ouzels (small diving birds). The bulk of a trout's diet, however, will be organisms that live in or along side the river or lake.

As availability of food types varies from each area and body of water, you cannot make a general statement as to which food is most important to trout. In many cases, foods most readily available to trout are insects. Knowing precisely which insect trout are targeting may seem only important to fly fishermen (as they must match their patterns to catch fish) and have little importance to gear or bait fisherman. Not so. On rivers, much of the time there are no prevailing insect hatches to distract trout. During these times trout will not be very selective, making them more open to striking lures or baits. The same is true for lakes. For both lakes and rivers, knowing which insect(s) trout are keying on and the insect's stage of development show you where in the lake or stream trout are feeding. This knowledge helps you find them, once

you have done that half the battle is won. For example, if trout are feeding on caddis larvae on the bottom of the river, presentations will be in that area; if trout happen to be rising for mayflies on the lake's surface, bait or lures will be most effective near the surface.

While insect hatches can sometimes make trout overly selective, preferring the numerous readily available bugs over any lure or bait, there are times of year when certain baits or lures are chosen by trout over insect imitations. For example, during fall on streams that have runs of salmon, trout target eggs that have fallen out of redds. During spring, when salmon fry are emerging from the same spawning areas, trout will target them. After periods of heavy rain earthworms washed into streams and lakes make easy meals for waiting trout. Windy days in late summer and early fall see grasshoppers blown into the water. During such times a single egg, small spinner or spoon, nightcrawler or grasshopper (in that order) will be the top trout enticers.

Regardless of the time of year or whether you are on lake or stream, knowing what trout are feeding on will show you where they are. This is one of the most important pieces of the puzzle to catching trout. In this chapter we will look at trout foods, from aquatic and terrestrial insects to foods available only during seasonal times. This will help you to better understand the behavior and availability of your quarry.

1) Aquatic

Aquatic organisms fall into two categories: those that live their entire lives beneath the surface, and those that live in water only during their larval stage. The great numbers of aquatic creatures available to trout, especially in lakes is too numerous to list in this book. Trout food sources featured here are those most common in lakes and streams, most recognizable by anglers and available to trout year-round.

Insects

The three most common and important aquatic insect families that trout fishermen must recognize are: the mayfly, caddisfly and stonefly.

Mayflies

Mayflies are probably the most familiar aquatic insect to trout fishermen. More abundant in streams than lakes, mayflies live in virtually all clean waters. They are found in both lakes and streams from sea level up to 11,000 feet. Being a delicate insect you won't find mayflies in streams or lakes that periodically dry up. The nymph of the mayfly, which can be found living in mud in lakes and clinging to and under stones in streams, is a knockout bait for trout when they can be collected or purchased. In Michigan streams, they are called "spring wigglers" and are one of the top baits for steelhead and large resident brown trout.

Mayfly nymphs are often very tiny, but the species fishermen recognize range from 1/2 to 1-1/2 inches long. Nymphs have 6 legs, a long abdomen and a long, thin 2 or 3 piece tail that may be as long as the body. They can be brown, with variances to black, yellow, or olive with lighter colored undersides. Mayfly nymphs are an excellent bait in spring and early summer when nymphs emerge from mud and rocks to travel to the surface to hatch. During these times the mayfly makes itself visible and available to trout.

Caddisflies

Caddisflies are the most numerous aquatic insect, especially in streams. Caddis hatches in warmer months are sometimes so voluminous that spent adult caddisflies can partially cover a lake shoreline. Caddisfly larvae are often found clinging to rocks in the shallows of streams and on edges of lakes near inlets and outlets. In the larval stage they are easily recognized by protective casings that shelter their fragile bodies. Caddis larvae build these casings with a sticky excretion that glues together tiny rocks, sticks, sand or whatever is available. They build a new case each time they grow. Sometimes they can be seen in large quantities in shallow portions of lakes and rivers with 10 feet of water or less. When carefully eased out of their casings caddisfly larvae are probably the best natural summertime bait for trout. When trout feed on caddis larvae they will eat casing and all. I'm sure this is what an Oregon summer steelhead had in mind when it swallowed the previously mentioned black ball-point pen cap.

Caddisfly larvae have four legs and a black head with body coloring ranging from brown, yellow, gray or green. They are commonly one to 1-1/2 inches in length, minus casing. Caddisfly larvae is an excellent bait year-round, but the best time for their use is during spring and summer months when larvae is largest.

Stoneflies

Stonefly nymphs look like mayfly nymphs and behave similarly. They have 6 legs, but unlike mayflies have rather short tails. The stonefly is more tolerant of pollution than the mayfly, and because of this can be found in a greater area. It is found living under rocks in streams and in muddy, shallow areas of lakes. The stonefly nymph is a hardy creature and when hooked properly stays alive for some time.

Stonefly nymphs vary in color, usually matching prevailing bottom color. They range from black, dark brown, olive and tan with a lighter underside coloring than the back.

Stonefly nymphs vary in size from one to 2 inches in length. Unlike mayflies and caddisflies that simply swim to the surface to emerge, stoneflies must crawl onto stream or lakeside rocks or vegetation to emerge as adults. Although found year-round in lakes and streams, the most effective times to use stonefly nymphs for bait is during summer months.

While generally the best time to use mayfly, caddisfly and stonefly nymph and larvae is previous to hatching, certain factors can bring on hatches sooner or later than normal. Low or higher water conditions, warmer than normal water temperatures, or rain and cloudy weather are some of the variables. Here, as in any other type of freshwater fishing, it pays to intimately know your water.

Crustaceans

Crustaceans, unlike aquatic insects, live their entire lives under water. Because of year-round availability, they are a primary food source of trout and make terrific baits. There are two types of freshwater crustaceans, both common to waters of North America and important to trout fishermen.

Crayfish

The crayfish (crawdad) is a smaller freshwater cousin of the lobster. Crayfish are identified by their two front pinchers, which if handled incorrectly inflict a painful nip on the fingers. They are prolific in both lake and stream, living under rocks, logs or other obstructions that provide shelter. The crayfish is a scavenger. Although the crayfish can grow to a length of 7 inches, those most commonly found by anglers are 2 to 4 inches long. Smaller ones, 1 to 2 inches long, make ideal baits, as they may be used whole. With larger crayfish, only meat inside the tail is used for bait. Depending on the size of crayfish, you will get one to three grayish-white baits out of each tail section. Large trout are especially fond of crayfish, trout over two pounds make them primary targets.

Crayfish are uniform in color, dark brown backs with hints of orange throughout and tinges of blue on the undersides. Capturing them by hand can be tricky, as they are capable of quick bursts of speed. There are, however, commercially available traps. Because of their availability, crayfish are an effective bait year-round.

Scuds

Scuds are a crustacean that resemble a large flea. Scuds are found primarily in lakes and their presence usually indicates larger trout are available. Lakes and impoundments that contain dense scud populations produce the fastest growing trout. Scuds inhabit lakes from sea-level to above 10,000 feet. Often too small for bait, scuds will reach a length of one inch, but most likely those you see will be 1/4 to 1/2 inch long. Scuds do not inhabit polluted water and are rarely found in water over 20 feet deep. The scud has a curved body with many individual plates, and approximately a dozen legs and appendages used for crawling, swimming and breathing. When observed swimming, their bodies are outstretched.

Scuds have a wide range of colorings including black, brown, grey, off-white and dull to bright red. Because they are available all year trout use scuds as a primary food source. Therefore, it is in the angler's best interest to find out if a favorite lake contains scuds; once you find scuds, you find trout.

Leeches

Not pretty to look at nor pleasant to handle these blood-sucking worms are trout favorites. While trout won't usually eat leeches in large quantities, they will not pass them up when available. Leeches are identified by flat, segmented bodies, small round mouths and a steady wave-like swimming motion. Although they live on land as well as in water, they are most frequently found in shallow lakes and streams. A leech can grow to 6 inches in length, but commonly are 2 to 4 inches long. An extremely tough bait, leeches remain on the hook until changed or eaten by a trout.

Leeches vary in coloring from black (most common shade), to brown, grey and dark green. Some have faint stripes or spots. Leeches are most active in spring, summer and fall.

Small Fishes (Forage Fish)

Sculpin

Sculpins, or "bullheads" as they are often called, are a favorite food of large trout. Sculpins are identified by two large round pectoral fins, heads that are wider than the rest of their bodies and two sharp "horns" above gill plates. Sculpins inhabit virtually all North American streams and lakes from sea-level to approximately 10,000 feet. The freshwater sculpin is a remarkably fast swimmer, darting from rock to rock, or under any place it can hide from predators. Sculpin are rarely seen laying out in the open. All trout species eat sculpins once they become large enough to swallow them, however, to the bull trout (Dolly Varden) of the West and big squaretail brook trout of northeastern Canada, sculpin is their main year-round diet. Sculpin reach a maximum of 6 inches, but the ones trout find most

appealing, and the best size for live bait, are the common one to 3 inches.

Sculpin range in color from black in glacial streams to mottled black/brown, brown and mottled dark green/black in clear lakes and rivers. They can be captured for live bait by using a small piece of earthworm on a tiny No. 14 hook, if hooked carefully sculpin will stay alive indefinitely.

Minnows

While the word "minnow" is synonymous with most small fish used for bait, such as chubs, shiners, roach, stickle-backs etc., there are also true minnows. All of the above are usually grouped in the "minnow" family of baits. Minnows of some species are common in almost all lakes, impoundments, rivers and streams. Minnows range in size from 1 to 3 inches, these are the best sizes to use for baits. Minnows catch trout year-round, especially larger trout that eat primarily bait fish. Minnows are most effective in spring and summer when they are numerous, water is still cold and few insects are hatching or available.

2) Terrestrials

Terrestrials are organisms that are born and live their entire lives on land. Terrestrials are important to trout fishermen because there are situations and times of year when these land-bound creatures find their way into streams and lakes. They wind up in water due to the whims of nature; they are blown onto water by winds, heavy rains wash them from on top of or under the ground, or they are careless in flight. There are thousands of terrestrials that inadvertently find their way into trout paths, but here, as with aquatics, we will only cover those most commonly found in lakes and streams.

Grasshoppers and Crickets

There is probably not a fisherman anywhere in trout country who has not seen a grasshopper or cricket fall off streamside foliage and be immediately sucked in by a waiting trout. Where grasshoppers are prolific trout key in, especially on windy days, from approximately mid-summer until the first freezes of late fall. Though more commonly found in tall grasses near streams than lakes, grasshoppers are an excellent bait in both types of water. Grasshoppers range in size from one-half to 2 inches in length.

Earthworms

Often known as leaf worms, nightcrawlers or dew worms, earthworms are unquestionably the most effective bait for trout in lakes or streams. While there are some Australian species of worms that grow to 5 feet long, most worms encountered by fish and fisherman will be one to 6 inches.

During and after periods of heavy rain, large numbers of worms are washed into rivers, or into tributary streams of lakes and impoundments. At these times worms are truly an unbeatable bait. The earthworm varies in color from pinkish to red to brown—sometimes all of these colors are on one worm.

3) Seasonal Foods

Salmon Eggs

As soon as a trout becomes large enough to swallow a single egg, it will eat each one it comes in contact with for the rest of its life. On Pacific coastal streams, and even lakes, eggs are common and often plentiful during fall salmon runs. From northern California to Alaska, inland to Idaho and on Great Lakes rivers and creeks, wherever spawning salmon can be found there will be rainbows, browns, cutthroat and Dolly Varden waiting for stray eggs to wash out of gravel redds. When large amounts of eggs are available, they become primary food sources for trout, much the same as during a major insect hatch. Eggs are a major food source from September through December. During these times trout concentrate in shallow riffles in streams, or near inlets and outlets of lakes, wherever salmon spawning takes place.

Salmon Fry

During spring and early summer months, over the same areas that are targeted for loose salmon eggs, trout feed on fry (baby salmon) as they gather for downstream migration. These tiny fish are 1/2 to 1 inch long, making a perfect bite-sized, high-protein morsel for larger trout. When trout key on fry, tiny spoons and spinners that imitate baby salmon are very effective. Watch for trout slashing through schools of the tiny fish. Stunned fish are eaten on the trout's next pass. Lake inlets and outlets can produce red-hot fishing during spring and early summer months as trout gather to intercept downstream traveling fry.

Chapter 3

Finding Trout in Lakes and Streams

Before discussing rods, reels, lines, baits and techniques, we must cover the most important aspect of trout fishing—the ability to locate your quarry by reading water, which is the ability to go to any lake or stream and apply given variables to determine where trout are hiding, resting or feeding. Once you have mastered this, you will be successful. One statement rings true anywhere trout are found. The angler with an old beat-up rod, dull hooks, dead bait and squeaky reel who is skillful at reading water will always outfish any angler with zero water reading abilities, even if that person has the best bait and state-of-the-art gear.

In this chapter we will discuss how to consistently find trout in lakes and streams. True, there are behavioral quirks that trout display that deviate from the norm, but there are definite patterns to finding trout that the angler may work with to up his catch ratio.

1) Reading Stillwaters: Lakes and Impoundments

Beginning trout fishermen along with a majority of experienced anglers are intimidated by lakes. Where in the expanse of featureless water will you find trout? Unlike a river or stream, where currents flowing around submerged objects give away fish holding structures, the still surface of a lake reveals little of what type of structure lies beneath. Lakes do require closer observation. A lake, like a river, has a physical makeup which tells anglers where trout are hiding and where their food will be.

The first step in reading a lake is not to look at the body of water as a whole, but to break it into sections, identifying changes in depth, structure, light and temperature.

Lake Zones

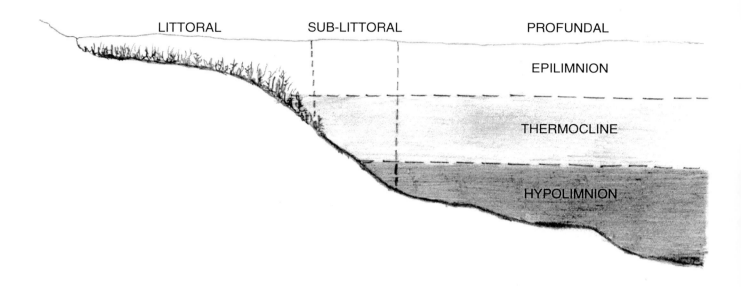

LITTORAL   SUB-LITTORAL   PROFUNDAL

EPILIMNION

THERMOCLINE

HYPOLIMNION

Lakes can be broken down into three zones determined by depth and each zone has an effect on where trout are found. These zones are the littoral, sublittoral and profundal.

The littoral zone is the portion of lake that begins at the shoreline and extends to the region where weeds no longer grow. Other littoral zones are shoals or submerged islands that support weeds. The littoral zone is the most important area to the trout fisherman, as most aquatic life lives in this area, thus attracting trout. Some lakes are shallow enough to support weed growth throughout, so their entire bottom qualifies as a littoral zone. Generally, shallow lakes are richer than steep lined, deep lakes and therefore have larger, healthier trout. The littoral zone depending on water clarity (light penetration stimulates plant growth), can reach to 30 feet deep.

The sub-littoral zone, though not as populated with aquatic life, still plays an important part for lake anglers. The sublittoral zone starts where plant life ceases. This is where the largest trout retreat when not prowling the shallower littoral zone for food.

The last area, the profundal zone, is the deepest portion of the lake. This area harbors zero plant life and consequently is a poor area to fish.

Once depth and zones have been established, look for fish holding and attracting structure. Start by making observations on your favorite lake. Take mental notes of all structure: inlet and outlet streams, drop-offs, weedbeds, sunken islands or shoals, submerged trees, springs, etc. Submerged structures in lakes can be fairly easy to spot as long as water is clear and the lake's surface is not too choppy. Scouting from a boat or high vantage point aids in spotting underwater structures. Local angling knowledge can be invaluable for learning lake structure. If the lake is popular learn all you can from other fishermen, guides and perhaps resorts. Doing this

cuts learning time in half and gets you into fish sooner. If the lake is remote or information on its structure is not available then look for the following keys to trout lakes:

Weedbeds: Always found in shallower portions of lakes, weedbeds attract important trout foods like aquatic insects, tiny forage fish as well as scuds and crayfish which in turn attract feeding trout. Weeds also provide shelter for trout. Although weeds can be a headache to fish near, as snags and fouled baits and lures can make fishing difficult, it pays to fish close to them. You will encounter two types of weedbeds when decoding lakes: weeds that float on the surface and weeds that are submerged. While it is possible with carefully placed casts to fish alongside floating weedbeds and minimize snagging, the best fishing will be just above submerged weeds.

Drop-offs: You don't need a boat to find drop-offs in lakes and reservoirs, simply look for areas where water color turns from dark to light. In clear, calm water conditions you can sometimes see the steep slope of a drop-off as it plunges into deeper water. Trout, larger trout especially, frequent these drop-offs to feed, having the security of deeper water close by.

Cliffs: Cliffs can provide some of the most consistent action on a lake. Cliffs attract trout because there are no perches for predators to work from, they can provide day-long shadows, insects may fall off the face directly into the water and feeding trout have an immediate escape route to deeper water. Cliffs can also provide a high point to survey the lake.

Springs: Springs are small underground streams that found their way up to the lake bottom. Springs provide many benefits to trout. They supply oxygen while ground water normally keeps a steady temperature year-round. During summer months when water temperatures may become uncomfortable for trout, springs provide cooler temperatures and oxygen. On the other hand, during winter, springs provide warmer water and oxygen. If you can locate springs in a weedbed, chances are you will find a good concentration of trout, as springs along with weeds provide shelter, food, comfortable water temperatures and oxygen. Springs are easy to locate; bubbles rising from the bottom give away their location.

Submerged Islands or Shoals: A shoal is a build-up of lake bottom that comes close to but does not reach the surface. Trout love these underwater islands for several reasons. They provide shallows where weeds may grow, attracting aquatic insects and other trout foods. Shoals also feature drop-offs which provide immediate access to deeper water where trout find security. Look for shoals where rock or gravel points gradually disappear into the water, or for a lighter colored bottom surrounded by darker water.

Submerged Trees and Overhanging Foliage: Downed trees provide shelter, shade and feeding stations for trout, as well as attracting aquatic insects. Overhanging trees and brush provide constant shade, slightly cooler water during summer heat, provide shelter from predators and attract terrestrial insects which sometimes fall into the lake.

Inlets, Outlets and Stream Channels: Inlets and outlets provide some of the best fishing a lake has to offer. During summer, an inlet stream brings cooler water temperatures, aquatic insects and oxygen. In fall months, inlet streams with runs of salmon carry loose salmon eggs into the lake. Trout also mill around stream mouths at the beginning of their spawning runs, waiting for an increase of water flow to trigger upstream migration. An outlet congregates aquatic life such as insects and tiny fish, due to the gradual pull of building currents toward the outlet. Unless there are underwater obstructions such as trees, large rocks or weeds, trout normally shy away from exposed outlets unless it is very early or late in the day.

An old stream-bed or channel in an impoundment can be a haven for trout, especially if the impoundment is fairly shallow. Old stream channels will be deeper, this translates into slightly cooler water temperatures in summer. Depressions in the bottom will sometimes hide trout.

Concentrate your efforts on shallower portions of the lake. Not only do shallow portions have plant life that attracts trout foods, the upper portions of the lake have the greatest exposure to light. Light is the primary energy source to start the food chain in lakes, and it also warms the water. The amount of light penetrating below the lake surface will tell at what depth trout will be. On cloudless days, for example, when lighting is at its most intense, insects, forage fish and trout seek out deeper water to escape sunlight. This is only true, however, if the water is calm. When the water surface is choppy from wind or other disturbances, light is refracted and trout stay near the lake's surface. When there are clouds present, trout stay near the upper portions of the lake, regardless of the condition of the lake's surface, assuming there is minimal boat traffic.

Knowing which trout prefer certain temperatures can help you find them in lakes if you are aware of the current water temperature. The temperature of a lake not only affects trout, but their foods as well. The effects of temperature change can tell you what time of day to fish, and also which techniques work best. To better understand this, let's look at what happens to the temperature of a common lake during the year.

Lakes are separated into three layers of temperature: epilimnion (top), thermocline (middle) and hypolimnion (bottom layer). In the spring, the epilimnion warms up, becoming less dense than the colder water beneath. This warm top layer varies in depth, relevant to overall depth and size of the lake. The epilimnion is where trout will be in spring and early summer. This layer receives the most oxygen through circulation by wind and waves, and also through sunlight.

The middle layer of water, the thermocline, is where the upper lake water ceases to circulate and begins to drop in temperature and oxygen content. Trout will "dip" into the thermocline to escape excessively warm upper lake temperatures during periods of hot weather.

The bottom layer of water, the hypolimnion, is the coldest portion of the lake. It harbors almost zero plant or fish life and has no oxygen content.

In fall months, when the water's surface begins to cool and the lake is basically the same temperature throughout, a "turn-over" occurs. Now that the lake is the same density, the water circulates like it did in spring and early summer. At this time, even the hypolimnion carries oxygen. This provides oxygen for trout during winter months. During winter, when colder water temperatures are found near the surface (in the epilimnion) trout are deeper than they were during spring, summer and early fall.

One of the most important pieces of equipment for a trout fisherman is a water thermometer. It only takes a few minutes to do a reading. Once you have taken a temperature measurement, you will be able to pinpoint at which level trout will be holding. Match that temperature with the other variables (lighting, structure and depth) and you will no longer be intimidated by "featureless" stillwaters.

2) Reading Flowing Waters: Rivers and Creeks

Trout that spend their lives in flowing water take up a position in the stream that fills three needs: shelter from predators, reasonably easy access to food and where the current offers the least amount of resistance. This depends largely on present water conditions. When trout fishing, you can assume that the majority of your fishing during the year will be done on rivers and creeks that are flowing clear. If this were the case (and it is approximately 90% of the time) finding trout in flowing waters would be fairly simple. However, prolonged periods of cold or hot weather and heavy rains are conditions that are also experienced. Knowing how trout respond to changes in water clarity, temperature and volume allow you to consistently hook fish all year.

We will look at different types of streams, how to recognize holding water and apply possible variables such as water volume, clarity and temperature to find trout.

There are basically two types of streams. The first is the medium to low gradient (slow-flowing) meandering "meadow" type. This stream has fairly uniform depth, scattered riffles and a bottom composed of small gravel, sand or silt. In these slower moving streams, trout cover is primarily undercut banks, overhanging grasses and downed trees. The second type is more commonly found in the West, that is the medium to high gradient (fast-flowing) stream with fast to moderate current. Bottoms in these streams consist of gravel and boulders and the physical makeup is pockets, pools,

riffles and runs. Defining holding water for trout in fast-flowing freestone streams is a bit more complicated than meadow streams.

When reading a trout river there is one constant: no two sections of river are exactly the same. Knowing this, there are several keys to the physical makeup of rivers that consistently show possible holding areas. "Possible" is a good term to use because often upon closer inspection what was first thought of as holding water does not meet holding water criteria.

In typical moderate to fast-flowing freestone streams, there are definite areas where you will not find trout. Rapids, waterfalls, chutes and steep, wide shallows are too swift and powerful or provide insufficient cover to hold trout. Trout need areas where they find comfort, security and easy access to food. When dealing with comfort a trout has to have a bottom composition of gravel, rocks or boulders without sand. Sand is a serious abrasive to gills, therefore trout avoid holding in sandy areas. If an area looks like bottom structure is predominantly sand, pass it up.

Unlike lakes, a river's surface gives away what type of bottom is present. If a river's surface is choppy or broken you can assume that bottom is made up of rock. A smooth water surface means a lack of obstructions for hiding areas, no escape from current, and bottom that is made up of tiny gravel, sand or silt. Trout gravitate to areas with rocks and boulders because they break up current, making it easier to hold without expending energy. When a river flows over or around a submerged large rock or boulder it causes a swirling boil, giving away a prime location for holding trout.

silt and sand.

Deadfalls (large trees or branches) that break up current are also good trout holding spots. Sunken trees not only break up current, they attract small forage fishes and aquatic insects. Also, look for current breaks or parting lines where fast water abrubtly changes to slower flow. Trout favor these breaks, where they can hold in slower portions on the edge of fast water. Here they are in an ideal position to dart in and out of the faster current to intercept insects or fish without burning a lot of valuable energy.

Since trout take the path of least resistance when seeking holding spots, you must look to areas where the river slows and begins to gain depth. These deeper areas can be of any size and length depending on amounts of water volume and physical makeup of the river. Other than pockets and eddies formed by midstream boulders and deadfalls, there are four specific types of holding water that form as they take shape below waterfalls, rapids and chutes:

Riffles: The area where rapids and chutes first start to slow down and gain depth. Riffles are characterized by bouncy, choppy water caused by refraction off boulders and rocks as the river slows.

Runs/Pools: Where riffles begin to calm and deepen, often this area is the deepest portion of holding water. Here the surface is not as turbulent, however it can still be slightly choppy or replaced by slicks and boils.

Tailouts: The area where the pool's depth starts to gradually lessen and shallow. Tailouts are normally wider than the rest of the holding areas, they are the slowest portion of the pool proper and are literally the tail-end of a classic piece of trout holding water.

Trout hold in eddies created by the boulder, either on the upstream side or more commonly, directly behind.

Another reason to look for areas of gravel, rock and boulders is that aquatic insects prefer these type of bottoms over

Break: The area directly after tailouts where the river again starts to speed up, shallow out and water turns from smooth to choppy. Breaks directly above rapids and chutes are prime trout holding areas.

Riffle-Run/Pool-Tailout-Break

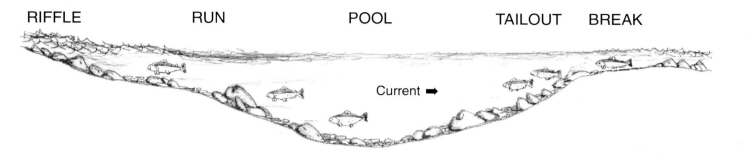

RIFFLE   RUN   POOL   TAILOUT BREAK

Current ➡

The "riffle-run/pool-tailout-break" configuration is the most common natural formation of holding water in a river, but it is only a generalization. Some stretches of trout water contain no more than the previously mentioned pockets and eddies behind boulders, or simply a riffle followed by a break. The one sure way to find trout when reading a fast flowing moderate to high gradient stream is to look for the flat spots. "Flats" are areas in holding water that have no downward (seaward) slope. They are areas that literally go up, or river bottoms gradually tilt upward. Remember no two stretches of holding water are alike, therefore these flats can be 2 feet to 200 feet in length, depending on the river's size. Flats generally occur most frequently where pool turns into tailout. At this point, the river bottom will slope upward. This upward slant provides trout with the slowest current. Flats can occur, however, anywhere in the river where there is sufficient cover for trout. The start of a tailout is an obvious flat, but they can be found in riffles, breaks, long deep runs, along a clay ledge, behind and in front of boulders, even in pockets of calm water inside fast water such as rapids and chutes.

Finding the flat spots can be fairly simple. When standing on a section of holding water, focus on the water line on the opposite bank. Follow water line contour as the run progresses downstream. You will notice that most of the holding area slopes downward, then at some point flattens out and flows somewhat level, or even tilted upward. These are the spots to concentrate on when reading a trout

river. Some stretches of holding water have more than one flat spot, some have none. These flatless places look good but are vacant of trout.

Now that you can identify holding areas, we have to examine water height and temperature to help locate trout in a river year-round.

Most stream fishing for trout is done in clear water conditions, which should make finding trout fairly simple with few variables to worry about. Fluctuating water conditions, however, are part of the year-round spectrum of trout fishing. With this in mind we have to understand how trout behavior changes under different water heights and clarity to consistently hook fish.

During winter rainy seasons, or during spring runoff, heavy flows will make 95% of the river too swift for trout to rest in and turn the river a dirty brown. Under these conditions trout seek out river edges close to the banks. This is the only portion of the river that allows them escape from heavy volumes and suspended silt. This water next to the bank is a degree less roily, having less suspended gill-clogging silt. These areas are not wide, only a few feet on average. Fishing will be poor, but short casts with a slow presentation into slower edges can still produce trout. With a foot or so visibility trout are holding remarkably shallow as cloudy water color gives trout a sense of security. Most of the time trout will be stressed under these conditions and it should be suggested not to fish until river levels stabilize and drop.

When rivers begin to drop they take on a brownish-green to a whitish-green color with approximately 12 inches of visibility. In the still heavy flows trout are hugging the banks in relatively shallow, calm current edges. Due to increased visibility trout are now able to find lures and bait.

Dropping from a foot of visibility to approximately 2 feet, there is still considerable water volume, but much less than previously. Water color will be dark olive green to emerald.

Tight edges of river are now wider, and tailouts are prime target areas for trout. The dark green color provides trout with a sense of security so they can travel fairly shallow when searching for food. Trout are often voracious during this stage, as it is usually the first opportunity to feed since high water.

When the river drops again there will be approximately 3 to 5 feet of visibility. Trout no longer feel safe in shallow, calm water because the canopy of green is for the most part gone. The edges and shallow tailouts that held trout are now void, except for periods of low light in early morning and evening when trout venture there to feed. The river still has a tint of color at this stage. The trout have moved to deeper holding water, preferring areas where the bottom is barely visible to where the choppy portion of the pool begins.

The final stage is normal to low flows with clear, unrestricted visibility. Trout now seek deeper water where the bottom cannot be readily seen, or gravitate toward water with a broken surface, normally at head-ins of pools in riffles, or lies that have broken water near a current break.

Temperature, along with degrees of visibility, has a great influence on trout behavior and where they hold. Temperature also dictates to trout when and where in holding water they feed. Now we will look at six different sets of temperatures and see how each affects trout behavior. By using a water thermometer, you will be able to tell where in the river trout hold when factored along with clarity and volume.

33 to 39 degrees: At temperatures less than 33 degrees trout become lethargic and non-responsive to bait and lures. When water is this cold, trout are found in the deepest and slowest water. In this slower, deeper water, temperatures are normally a degree or two warmer and the need for oxygen is not as important because metabolism has been slowed by the cold. Trout caught under these cold conditions are normally poor fighters.

40 to 44 degrees: Trout will still hold in slower, deeper water on current edges in these temperatures. Not only do trout start to become active when temperatures reach 40 plus degrees, these are temperatures when aquatic insects, crustaceans and tiny fish also start to move about. Sea-run trout begin to move upriver in these temperatures. In clear water conditions it becomes tricky pinpointing holding trout. They are still in deep, slow water, but due to the slightly warmed water they may also be found at the end of broken riffles and choppy runs of moderate depth, especially later in the day after limited winter sun has had a chance to warm the water a few degrees. When water is inside 40 to 44 degrees it pays to work everything that qualifies as holding water.

45 to 50 degrees: Trout show the greatest increase in activity in this range due to warmer water and the increase in aquatic life movement. Trout now gravitate towards areas of river with more flow, leaving dead water for areas with more dissolved oxygen. Trout now lay in tailout breaks, in the slightly faster water on current breaks, parting lines and in choppy head-ins and runs. Sunlight now starts to become a factor as trout retreat to more broken water as lighting increases.

51 to 60 degrees: These temperatures represent the trout's range of maximum activity and hatches are triggered of aquatic insects. Crustaceans and small fish also show the greatest amount of activity. Trout now respond best to baits and lures and fight their hardest. Under these temperatures trout seek out flats in areas of depth with broken water. The deeper, slower sections will not have enough oxygen nor cover, and trout only venture there during night or in hours of dim light to feed. The choppy water contains more oxygen.

61 to 65 degrees: This range is the top end of optimum trout activity. Oxygen levels are now concentrated in upper portions of holding water where only choppy water is cool enough and contains enough dissolved oxygen for trout comfort. Sea-run trout cease movement at these temperatures and resident trout become extremely sensitive to lighting. The best fishing to be found on days when the temperature reaches 65 degrees is early morning and late evening when water temps are lower and there is less direct lighting to spook fish.

65 to 70 degrees: Other than brown trout and certain species of desert rainbows, these temperatures are the beginning of discomfort for trout. Most aquatic activity ceases and oxygen is severely depleted when water reaches the 70 degree mark. Playing trout, and especially releasing them, under these temperatures is an iffy proposition as trout are difficult to revive after expending themselves in warm water. It is best to wait for cooler days or rain to drop water temperatures before fishing.

Remember, ability to read flowing waters means being able to recognize what physically makes up holding water along with factoring the variables of water volume, clarity and temperature. Learn these and you will consistently catch trout regardless of your chosen technique.

Chapter 4

The Tools for Trout

The first three chapters introduced you to North American trout, what they eat and where to find them in lakes and streams. Now that we are familiar with our quarry we now have to assemble an outfit that gives the greatest ease of use, greatest sport and durability. Rods, reels and lines are tools of the trade for the trout fisherman. Which ones are best for you? In reality there are a thousand variations of trout outfits. Keep in mind, as with technique, there is no one combination of line, rod and reel that will suffice for all trout fishing. Our goal here is to suggest which combinations work best for small streams, rivers and lakes, whether for casting lures or bait, trolling or still-fishing.

Rods

The considerations for determining the correct rod are choosing techniques, determining the size of trout common in those waters and then matching rods to fit those variables. The most important criteria for choosing a rod are length and action. The material a rod is made from has no bearing on its

ability to catch trout. Arguing which material is better is really a moot point. Save for a few obvious advantages, such as the lightness of graphite composite rods, it is entirely up to fishermen to judge which rod feels best.

Each rod is designed to handle specific weights when cast, these weights translate to lures and bait. When you go beyond these limits, such as a lure that is too heavy for the blank or a bait that is too light, what happens? The rod will not perform. For example, too heavy a lure causes over-flexing, lost accuracy, shorter casting distances and perhaps damage to the blank while too light a lure or bait will not load up the rod, or sufficiently create enough bend to transfer power to propel a cast.

When we discuss rods for trout fishing assume that each time "rod" is mentioned it will be a spinning style rod. All methods and techniques for trout fishing are practiced with spinning reels (exceptions being level-wind reels used for trolling heavy gear and fishing large rivers for big fish). This is because the majority of all trout fishing is done by casting tiny lures and bait. Spinning-style rods have larger "hoop" type guides near the reel seat that allows line to leave the spool friction-free when casting.

Whether your rod is a conventional spinning type or a casting/trolling style, be sure it has the correct number of guides. A good rule of thumb is to have one guide for every foot of rod. For example, if the rod is eight and a half feet long, it should have no fewer than eight guides. Too few guides put unnecessary pressure points on line when playing fish. This increases friction on the line, weakening it. The more guides a rod has, the more evenly line follows the rods' bend. This feature is important when trout fishing due to ultralight lines commonly used.

Choose a rod that feels comfortable. For example, when tennis

players choose a racquet they want one that has a comfortable grip. You will be holding your rod longer in a day than a tennis player would hold a racquet during a match. A comfortable, relaxed grip helps eliminate fatigue. Commercially manufactured rods come with two types of handles: natural cork or foam. Foam provides a better grip and like cork is warm to the touch on cold days, however cork may be sanded to custom fit anglers' hands.

Types of rods best suiting different situations

For small streams and trout that may range up to a pound, a short, ultralight rod is the choice. For length, consider whether the stream is fairly open, like a meadow stream, or surrounded by trees and brush. Open streams without foliage to restrict casting motions allow the use of a longer rod, from 6-1/2 to 9 feet long. The longer rod not only allows you to cast tiny lures and small bait a greater distance, it also has these advantages: it allows you to keep back from the water's edge to prevent spooking trout and keep more line out of the water to avoid drag. Line drag causes lures and bait in flowing water to unnaturally speed up and excess bow in the line causes loss of feel and control. Small streams with an abundance of trees and bushes lining the banks do not allow freedom of movement with longer rods. In these situations shorter rods 4 to 5 feet long are easier to maneuver in and out of brush and do not need as much room for a backcast.

For relatively small trout found in streams or situations in lakes and streams where extremely wary fish require gossamer lines or long casts with petite bait and lures, you want a ultralight rod to accommodate them. All commercially-made rods and blanks purchased for rod building have line pound test ratings and suggested lure weights labeled near the butt section. If you have chosen a short or long rod for small streams and/or flighty fish, choose one with

line ratings of 2 to 4 or 2 to 6 pound test and a lure weight rating of 1/32 to 1/4 ounce. This extremely light blank allows you to use light monofilaments, cast the smallest bait and lures with distance and still get maximum sport from trout ranging from 6 to 15 inches. The rod's wispiness gives you the chance to land a larger trout should you encounter one.

If you can only use one rod for all types of trout fishing, it should be a 6 to 7 foot long medium action spinning style, have a pound test rating of 4 to 12 and a lure rating of 1/4 to 3/8 or 1/4 to 5/8 ounce. With this rod you may be compromising length for casting distance and heaviness in the butt section when using ultralight lines, etc., but it has enough "middle ground" features for use in small streams and ponds up to large trout rivers and lakes. It has reserve power in the butt section to cast a heavier lure and set a hook, enough flexibility in the tip section to softly lob a delicate bait and detect the slightest nibble, can handle trout up to double-digit poundage, as well as adequately show off the scrappiness of a 10-incher. This rod is a good choice for travel when bringing half a dozen rods is not practical. Besides its all-purpose features, a rod of 6-1/2 to 7 feet, rated 4 to 6, 4 to 8 or 4 to 10 with a lure rating of 1/4 to 5/8 ounce is ideal for large streams, small rivers and the majority of lakes and impoundments.

When employing downriggers while lake trolling for large trout, it is possible to use almost any style, length and weight of rod. However, lake trolling usually involves a diving lure of some kind like a Flatfish, Kwikfish, Hot-Shot, Wee Wart, etc., which creates a large degree of pull to impart action to the lure and make it dive. Gang trolls, weighted spinners and spoons also resist water. Without the aid of a downrigger when using these lures, rods must have sufficient backbone not to over-flex. Trolling heavier gear requires a heavier rod. A 7-1/2 to 9 foot rod rated for 6 to 10 to 8 to 12 pound lines have enough "pack" in the butt sections to pull a diving lure without over-flexing, yet are supple enough to allow trout to show off their fighting skills.

Reels

When purchasing a reel, regardless of style, look for the following keys: a smooth drag and quality workmanship. A velvet-smooth drag is the most important part of your reel. Since you will be using light lines for the majority of your fishing, the reel must "let go" of the line without a jerky pull when trout take off for the horizon. Even small trout can snap lines easily when the drag sticks, especially if you are fishing in current or the trout lunges away on a short line. You get what you pay for, cheaper reels usually have inconsistent drag systems. When these cheaper drags are set tight, no line can escape the spool, but when they are lightened up the drag slips too much.

Match your reel to the rod you will be using. You have often heard the term "balanced outfit", this simply means matching an ultra light reel with a light action rod, medium reel with a medium action rod, and so on.

Quality workmanship is evident the minute you pick up a reel and spin the handle. It should spin solidly and smoothly. If you have doubts about the quality of a reel, there are many brands known for their quality. Mitchell, Eagle Claw, Shimano, Zebco, Penn, Shakespeare, Daiwa, Johnson and Ryobi are names that are well-known for producing quality reels. If care is taken not to jar them excessively and they are lubricated yearly, a reel will last through years of steady use.

Trout fishermen have three styles of reels to choose from: closed face, open faced and casting. Each style serves a different purpose. Let's look at each style individually and show why you would choose one over the other.

Closed Face Reels

For a youngster or a beginner of any age, the closed face reel is possibly the best choice simply because they are the easiest reel to use and they are the least expensive. To cast, depress the button on the rear to disengage the pin holding line on the spool, as the rod is swung outward the thumb is let off and line is released. A practically foul-proof design, due to the line being completely encased in a cover, make the closed face the best reel for entry-level trout anglers. The center opening in the cone-shaped cover also allows line to enter the first rod guide at a lesser angle than spinning reels.

Closed face reels, despite their ease, have some minor drawbacks. Their retrieve ratio (the amount of line coiled on the spool for each revolution of the reel handle) is less than spinning reels. Since line must be forced through the center opening the resulting friction reduces casting distance. By using lighter lines you can overcome this short casting handicap, but due to friction, closed face reels can wear out light lines quickly. It is important to remember to change light lines often when using closed face reels.

Open Face Reels

Open faced spinning reels are the most popular reels used by trout fishermen. They have higher retrieve ratios, allow for longer casts with light lures and bait and have larger capacity spools. By hanging below the rod, spinning reels are positioned by gravity and do not have to be held upright

Closed face spinning reel.

Open face spinning reel.

Level wind casting reel.

A properly presented spinner tricked this Dolly Varden.

like a closed face or level wind. When fishing all day this translates as less wrist fatigue.

Open faced reels are not as foul-proof as closed face, as line must be gathered onto the spool with a small amount of tension to avoid loose coils that may leap off the spool and foul casts. For the best performance from your spinning reel, fill the spool to within 1/8th inch of the rim. When line is properly loaded in this manner, open face reels will perform their best. You will achieve maximum casting distance and retrieve more line per revolution of the handle.

An ideal all-purpose reel for trout fishermen is a spinning reel that handles small to medium-sized lures and casts efficiently large unweighted or tiny weighted baits. It should have a skirted spool to prevent line from getting under the spindle and have an approximate capacity for 150 yards of 6 pound test. Line capacity is normally printed on sides of spinning reel spools.

Drag systems on open faced reels vary. Some are located on top of the spool, some are positioned at the rear. Each system has pros and cons, in the end it's the angler's choice. Rear drags are easier to get at while fighting fish but it requires a glance away from the rod to determine which way to turn the knob. Front drags are more durable and more easily manipulated, however you must reach around your mainline to adjust. Regardless of which one you choose, be sure the drag is butter smooth.

A tip to remember: when playing fish with spinning reels, either closed or open faced, be sure the spool is not revolving when reeling line in. If you see the spool spinning as you are reeling (you will hear the drag buzzing and clicking) the drag is too loose and no line is being gathered onto the spool. What this does is put a twist in the line for each revolution of the spool. Line twist severely weakens line and makes it unmanageable during casting.

Level Wind Reels

When trout fishing, level wind reels are used only infrequently. They are more suited for large salmon and steelhead, but they do have a small niche for trouters. Because of the need for weight to pull line off the spool when casting and the fact that light lines are back-lashed easily, level winds are not popular. Any lure or bait weighing less than 1/4 ounce cannot be cast accurately or without causing spool overrun. They do have superior drag systems and are the choice when trolling diving lures, spoons, weighted spinners and gang trolls.

When trolling with level wind reels it is easier to feed line off the spool until desired trolling depth is reached. The level wind bar, or line leveler, allows fishermen to count the amount of line being let out by each back and forth pass of the bar. This makes it easier to return to the approximate depth where trout are striking.

Lines

There are many brands of premium monofilament available to trout anglers. Choose one that fits the needs of your favorite water.

Having a balanced, matching rod and reel is very important for trout fishing. However, even the highest quality rod and reel will not help when matched with a poor quality line. Monofilament lines are working tools for trout fishermen. When choosing a line, regardless of brand, always purchase premium monofilaments. High quality lines are more expensive for good reasons: they have uniform diameter, resist deterioration and are much stronger. Saving a few dollars by buying lower grade lines may be justified in the pocketbook, but poor knot strength, low abrasion resistance and lost fish are not.

Trout fishermen today have better quality lines than ever to choose from. Early post-war monos were not reliable as they were not uniform in diameter, were too stiff to be cast efficiently and were brittle. Today, improvements in chemistry have produced lines that are thinner, stronger and available in colors ranging from bright fluorescent blue, green and gold to subtle tones of green, brown, pink and clear. Today's lines have superior knot strength, tensile strength, flexibility, half the memory and have varying qualities of stretch and limpness.

When choosing a premium monofilament you will find some lines are "stiff" while others are "limp." Limp monos are the usual choice for trout fishing, they work best for casting light lures and bait. When fishing bait, limp lines give the bait a more natural, uninhibited movement, plus trout cannot feel limp lines as easily as stiff ones when they pick up a bait. Limp lines have less memory which means they are less likely to form coils that may leap off the spool at inopportune times, causing tangles or cutting down casting distance. Limp mono does nick and abrade easier, so it must be changed more often. Stiff monos have a harder finish that resists abrasion, but are too rigid for trout fishing.

Lines for trolling, however, should be stiffer as hard finished lines resist twisting from rotating lures such as spoons and spinners and absorb shock from strikes better. When using downriggers, hard lines are a necessity when snapping lines in and out of releasing clips.

The most common and useful lines for all trout fishing are 4, 6 and 8 pound test. These line weights handle most trout between 6 and 20 inches and cast a wide range of light lures and bait. There will be times when you must drop

down to 2 pound when using tiny lures and bait for wary fish in air-clear water, but extreme patience and an ultra-smooth drag is a necessity in order to land a trout. When trout fishing the lighter the line the better the results, especially when bait fishing.

Read labels on premium monofilaments carefully. Since fishermen usually buy lines by pound test rather than diameter, one line can break at a greater variance than another. For example, some lines break at 6 pounds, while another "6 pound test" may break at over 10 pounds. Manufacturers by law must produce a line that breaks no less than labeled, so they give lines a bit more diameter to be certain of the claim. Look for lines that have the lowest diameter for true pound test ratings.

For 95 percent of all situations when stream fishing or stillfishing in lakes, 75 to 100 yards of line is sufficient. To prevent wasting expensive line fill the spool up partially with an inexpensive, slightly heavier test backing and fill the spool to capacity with the "working" 75 to 100 yards of premium line. Keep the spool full—this allows you to cast farther and gather more line on the spool with each turn of the reel handle.

When choosing line color assume that most of your fishing will be done under clear water conditions. Fluorescent lines are a great advantage when following your presentation around rocks and obstructions in rivers, also when trolling in low light. However, in clear conditions bright monos may scare off trout. Since watching your line is an important consideration, the suggestion must be made to stick with a clear monofilament. Subtle green and brown

monos camouflage well, so well in fact that a fisherman cannot follow his line. This can be a disadvantage when trying to pinpoint casts. Natural colored lines can also cost you fishing time. With monos that disappear into the glare there is no way of knowing if you have worked the same area twice. Clear monos can be followed visually yet are not perceived by trout.

If you feel more comfortable using fluorescent monos you may still employ them in clear water if you color the first several feet of line from your lure with a black, waterproof marking pen. Running the marker up and down the line will camouflage the fluorescent color.

Check your line often when fishing, if it feels nicked or braided or twists when tension is released, replace it with fresh line. Playing a lot of trout, stretching the line from breakoffs, losing line from those breakoffs or constant retying means immediate replacement. New line not only casts farther, it has greater knot strength and is stronger, especially ultralight lines of 2, 4 and 6 pound. One nick in these lines lowers pound test capacity by half. To save money, purchase line in large capacity spools, the more you buy the better price you receive.

A few other tips about monofilament. Line is especially sensitive to UV radiation and prolonged exposure to heat. Store spools of line in dark, cool areas and keep reels out of car trunks and back windows where sunlight can get to them. Also, when tying knots in monofilament, be sure to wet knots before cinching them tight with a bit of saliva or water. Use slow, even tension when tightening knots; quickly tightening dry knots burn and weaken line.

Chapter 5

Techniques

We know how to identify trout, their primary foods, where to locate them in lakes and streams and have chosen a balanced outfit. Now we take this knowledge one step further and apply it to techniques. For each given circumstance on trout water, there will always be one technique that out produces another. Your job is to determine which one of the following is most effective. This is done by applying knowledge absorbed through the first three chapters. By putting together all variables in lakes and streams—lighting, temperature, existing foods, structure and water clarity—you will be able to find trout and apply proper techniques.

Please keep in mind that the only way to determine proper techniques is on-the-water-experience. There are no shortcuts. By intimately learning your chosen lake or stream you will become familiar with proper techniques for all variances in conditions at all times of year. What it boils down to is experimentation. However, the most alluring aspect of trout fishing is that rarely in the course of a season will you experience identical conditions. It's the myriad of variables and constant challenge that brings us back to trout waters time and again.

Lake Trolling

Trolling for trout in lakes may appear simple, but it's not as easy as it looks. Like any other technique it requires experimentation to find the right combinations. Trolling is the best way to cover the greatest amount of water in a shorter time, exposing your lure to large amounts of fish.

We'll start with trolling speeds. Since there is no way to gauge exact miles per hour due to variables of wind, how fast you row, how slow your motor trolls, etc., optimum speeds for trolling will be directly related to action imparted to the lure(s) you are using. Place your lure next to the boat and watch its action. Adjust your motor or rowing speed until lure action is satisfactory and maintain that speed as close as possible.

Start trolling where you expect trout to station. In the majority of lakes this is close to shorelines, as those are the zones where most trout foods are located. Begin trolling near shorelines and gradually work outward. This is not an absolute, as there may be abrupt changes in depth and bottom structure. Here again it pays to know your chosen body

of water intimately. A depth finder eliminates much guess work and will show you precisely where drop-offs, shoals, underwater points and perhaps depth of holding trout. However, starting near shore and working outward is a solid way to begin trolling.

Choosing proper trolling depth can be difficult. We will assume that you do not have the aid of downriggers that practically eliminate error. When possible, the angler should have two rods out, each set at different levels. If strikes are frequenting one rod over the other, you can change the other rod to the same depth. Temperature is a major factor in determining trolling depth. A rule to follow is if surface temperatures are between 50 and 60 degrees, alternate trolling depths between a few feet down to 10 feet. If surface temperatures are 65 degrees or better, troll deeper than 10 feet.

The amount of line out affects depth. A good starting point is to troll between 30 and 50 feet behind the boat. Doing this has a double advantage. One, if you are using a motor, trout cannot hear you and aren't spooked by noise. Two, this amount of line allows lures to work at optimum depth as designed. Less line than 30 feet will not allow some diving plugs to achieve maximum depth, while more than 50 feet causes the "push" of water resistance against the line to make lures, regardless of design, rise.

One sure method to cover more depth levels is to troll in an irregular "S" pattern. This is done by simply turning the boat to the left and to the right. By doing this, trollers can change lure depth and speed without changing the amount of line out or altering trolling speed. For example, if your rod is positioned on the left side of the boat, upon making a left turn the lure slows down its action and either drops deeper or floats upwards, depending on design. Conversely, by making a right turn, lure speed increases causing it to rise if it is a revolving lure, such as a spoon or spinner, or dive deeper if it is a plug.

Your line diameter has a direct effect on trolling depth. The thicker the line, the shallower the lure runs. This is due to line thickness in relation to water resistance. The thicker the line, the more "push" upwards. Thinner, lighter lines have less resistance, allowing lures to work and dive deeper. Because trout tend to strike trolled lures with an immediate, forceful yank, line should test no lighter than 6 pound to absorb shock, yet not heavier than 12 pound to allow lures to gain depth and not spook fish.

Again, experimentation with trolling speeds, different lures and the amount of line out determine depth. The key is to determine where in the lake trout hold by temperature, structure, lighting and food availability, then troll as close as possible to those areas and depths.

Trolling is a lure fisherman's domain. Rarely does a lure have to be fished deeper than 25 feet when trolling, as long as the majority of foods are in the top layer of water. Whenever there is surface chop or waves, trout will be found feeding just below the chop. Low levels of light penetrating the waves bring up light sensitive scuds and other tiny aquatics, followed by baitfish and trout in hot pursuit. A prime example is 100 mile long Kootenay Lake in British Columbia. Its giant species of Gerrard rainbow average 10 pounds, commonly reach 20 and each year several around 30 pounds are landed. Guides there do not bother to fish unless there are waves on the lake, then they troll large fish-imitating bucktails on the surface. The bigger the chop, the better the fishing.

When using correct speeds and amount of line out, you should not have to add weight to lures to achieve these depths. For this reason, three basic lures suffice for trolling: spinners, spoons and plugs. These three lures can be interchanged at any time when trolling to achieve proper depth, lure size, degree of action, color or matching existing foods.

A tip to remember: the most well presented lure means nothing if hooks are not kept sharp. It's that "sticky-sharpness" that gets nipping, short-striking fish and keeps trophy trout on the line.

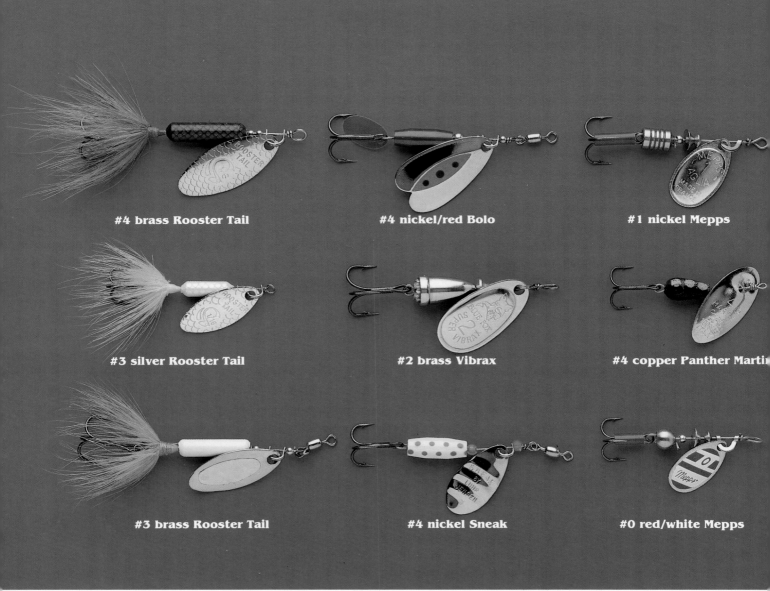

#4 brass Rooster Tail

#4 nickel/red Bolo

#1 nickel Mepps

#3 silver Rooster Tail

#2 brass Vibrax

#4 copper Panther Martin

#3 brass Rooster Tail

#4 nickel Sneak

#0 red/white Mepps

Weighted spinners used for trolling or casting in streams

Trolling Spinners

There are six practical sizes of spinners for trout fishing: No. 00, No. 0, No. 1, No. 2, No. 3 and No. 4. (No. 00 being smallest and No. 4 largest.) Spinners are commercially made two ways: with brass weighted bodies and unweighted decorative plastic. Judging how deep spinners work is first done by body weight and secondly by blade size.

Unweighted spinners, such as Colorados or Hildebrandts, trolled at approximately 40 feet are working at 3 to 6 feet deep. Weighted spinners like Mepps, Rooster Tails, Vibrax, Panther Martins, Sneaks and Bang Tails from 1/12 to 1/3 ounce in sizes No. 0 to No. 4 run 6 to 15 feet deep. Believe it or not, 1/2 ounce spinners run deeper with small No. 2 blades than with No. 4's due to smaller blades having less water resitance and less tendency to plane upwards. With that in mind you can troll a 1/4 ounce No. 2 at the same depth as a 1/2 ounce No. 4.

The first key to trolling spinners is to carefully watch the speed of the blade spin. Spinners work on the premise of one flash emitting from the blade per revolution. For the spinner to work at its optimum, blade spin must be kept to a minimum. A slow blade spin has a higher degree of flash than a rapid one. More trout are attracted from a greater range with slow blade spin than a rapid one. Two to three revolutions per second is about perfect when trolling spinners. Be aware, however, that slow blade spin is possible only in larger sizes of trout spinners, sizes 3 to 4. Small spinners have rapid blade spin regardless, just do your best to keep revolutions slow as possible.

When choosing color and size for spinners, remember that a spinner resembles nothing in the food chain. It is simply an attractor. With that in mind, lighting and water temperature determine colors. Early morning, late afternoon/evening, dark cloudy days, colder water (surface temperatures, below 45 degrees) and low water visibility

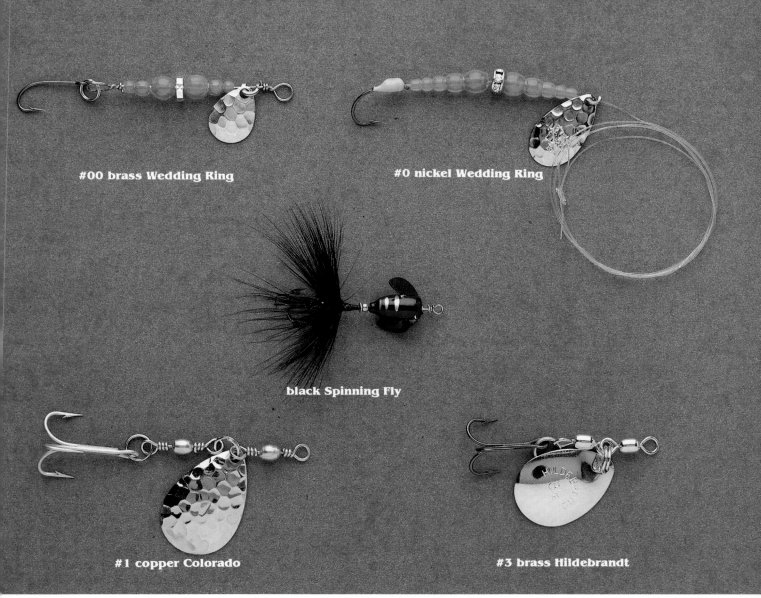

#00 brass Wedding Ring

#0 nickel Wedding Ring

black Spinning Fly

#1 copper Colorado

#3 brass Hildebrandt

Unweighted trolling spinners

require more flash to attract and excite trout, so silver-plated blades are desireable under these conditions. Silver—not nickel—creates the greatest amount of trout attracting flash. silver-plated spinner blades reflect 90 percent of all light, while nickel, even though it appears shiny, absorbs light and surrounding color, appearing almost black to trout. Nickel does work well, however, in clear water and bright, cloudless days. Brass is the best choice when you are not sure of conditions, when overcast, in slightly tinted water or when surface temperatures are above 55 degrees.

When trolling revolving lures like spinners be sure to use a quality ball-bearing swivel placed several feet above the lure to prevent line damaging twisting.

Trolling Spoons

Unlike spinners, spoons actually resemble baitfish in shape and action. Trout anglers have two choices for trolling spoons: the standard casting style and thin-bladed. Standard casting styles are fine when fan casting stationed in a boat or on shore. These spoons are thicker and must be trolled at faster speeds than thin-bladed trolling styles in order to impart the same action. Because of their thin profile the same action is imparted to them at half the speed it would take to obtain the same from a casting style spoon.

When trolling spoons proper speeds vary with each style and shape of spoon. In order to achieve trout-appealing swimming action from spoons, the spoon must wobble from side to side and not spin. There are three reasons for doing this. One, when a spoon wobbles, it gives off a higher percentage of flash than when it spins. Two, a side-to-side wobble more closely resembles a baitfish. A tightly spinning spoon resembles nothing and does not look natural. Three, when a spoon spins, it increases its buoyancy and is forced toward the surface. Test each type and spoon style along side the boat to achieve ideal wobble before letting out line to troll.

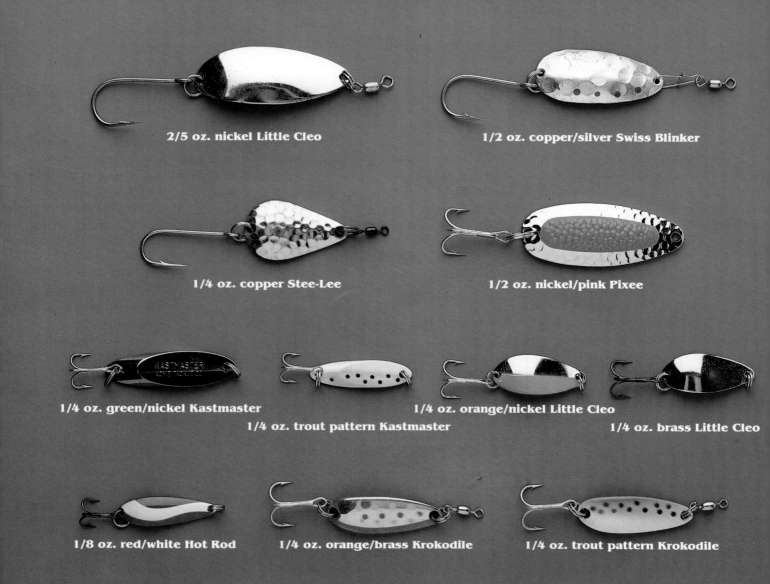

2/5 oz. nickel Little Cleo

1/2 oz. copper/silver Swiss Blinker

1/4 oz. copper Stee-Lee

1/2 oz. nickel/pink Pixee

1/4 oz. green/nickel Kastmaster

1/4 oz. trout pattern Kastmaster

1/4 oz. orange/nickel Little Cleo

1/4 oz. brass Little Cleo

1/8 oz. red/white Hot Rod

1/4 oz. orange/brass Krokodile

1/4 oz. trout pattern Krokodile

Weighted trolling and casting spoons

When choosing spoons for trolling, in casting (weighted) styles look for these shapes as they closely resemble baitfish in profile and action: the "classic" styles such as Dardevles, Wonder Lures, Krocodiles, Pro Lures and Pixies and "oval" styles like Thomas Cyclones, Little Cleos, Devle Dogs, B.C. Steels and Johnson Silver Minnows.

For thin-bladed trolling styles Canadian Wonders, F.S.T.'s, Dick Nites, Needlefish and Triple Teasers are the choices. Spoons for trolling should be 1-1/2 to 3 inches long, these lengths represent the sizes of baitfish commonly sought by trout. However, if you find that trout in your chosen body of water are taking baitfish larger or smaller, adjust spoon size accordingly. Ideal weights for trolling spoons are 1/8, 1/4, 1/2 and 2/5 ounce.

Thin-bladed spoons must have weight added in order to achieve depth. Thin-bladed spoons trolled without added weight run 3 to 6 feet down when set 30 to 50 feet back, with depth depending on present trolling speed. One-eighth and 1/4 ounce bead chain keel trolling sinkers are ideal when set 3 to 4 feet up from the spoon on the main-line. These keel trolling sinkers put a thin-bladed spoon at 10 to 25 feet, again depending on trolling speed, weight of sinker and amount of line out.

Colors for spoons depend upon current conditions and type of baitfish present. For early morning/evening, low water visibility, cold surface temperatures below 45 degrees and dark, cloudy days a silver-plated body is the choice. If trout are keying on small perch or trout as feed, spoons painted with these designs are the choice, as long as the lake is clear enough or these natural colors will be neutralized in darker water. Nickel finishes and some metallic finishes such as blues and greens work well in exceptionally clear water or on bright, cloudless days. Brass colored bodies are a good choice when you are unsure of conditions or presence of baitfish. Many brands of thin-bladed spoons have fluorescent orange or red

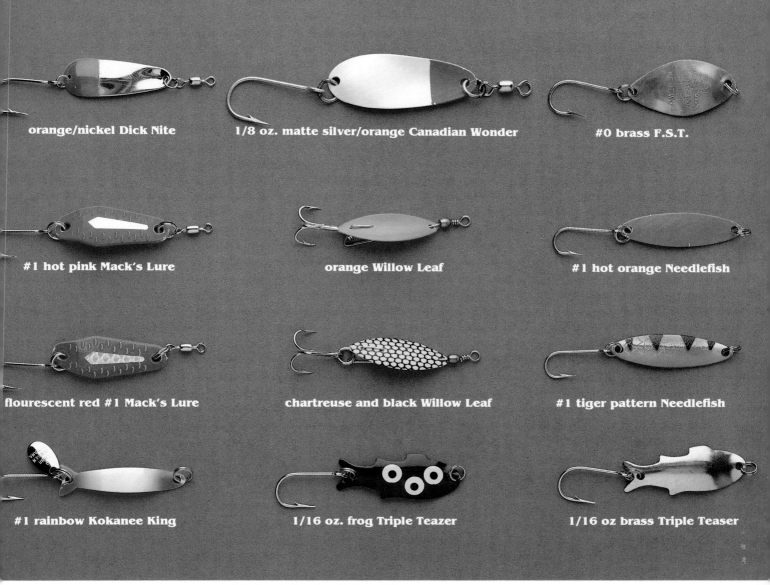

orange/nickel Dick Nite

1/8 oz. matte silver/orange Canadian Wonder

#0 brass F.S.T.

#1 hot pink Mack's Lure

orange Willow Leaf

#1 hot orange Needlefish

flourescent red #1 Mack's Lure

chartreuse and black Willow Leaf

#1 tiger pattern Needlefish

#1 rainbow Kokanee King

1/16 oz. frog Triple Teazer

1/16 oz brass Triple Teaser

Thin-bladed trolling spoons

heads and these added bright colors can sometimes trigger strikes when natural and plain bright metal finishes are not producing.

Trolling Plugs

Many veteran trout trollers claim plugs produce more large fish. This statement is probably true, as plugs more closely resemble baitfish than spinners or spoons.

Plugs are designed to rapidly wobble when trolled. What separates one style of plug from another is degree of wobble. Some plugs have a tight wobble, vibrating in a short space while others have an animated side to side action as wide as the plug body itself. Some plugs are designed to float and dive when pulled, some have neutral buoyancy while others are weighted to sink.

Floating plugs, such as Hot-Shots, Hot-n-Tots and Wee Warts have a tight wobble, while floating banana-shaped plugs like Flatfish and Kwikfish have wider wobbles than other style plugs. These floating plugs dive when trolled from 4 to 20 feet deep depending on the size plug. A general rule of thumb is larger floating plugs dive deeper than smaller ones. Banana-shaped plugs are the only styles that do not dive, so if you want to fish them more than a few feet down you must add a keel sinker. Deep diving neutral buoyancy or sinking plugs, such as Rebels and Rapalas run 15 to almost 30 feet.

Because plugs so closely resemble baitfish, colors and sizes should come as close as possible to present ones in the lake. Natural perch, crayfish, frog or trout colored plugs are good choices in clear water conditions and work well in all temperature ranges. If the water is cloudy to a degree with limited visibility you may want to choose contrasting plug colors, such as black back/white belly, black back/gold sides or black back/silver sides. Plugs of 1-1/2 to 4 inches long should represent all sizes of baitfish you

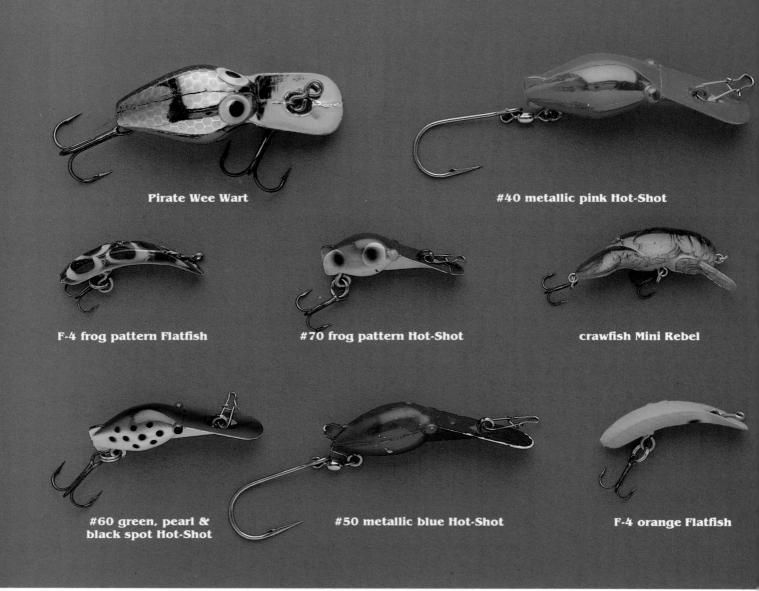

Pirate Wee Wart

#40 metallic pink Hot-Shot

F-4 frog pattern Flatfish

#70 frog pattern Hot-Shot

crawfish Mini Rebel

#60 green, pearl & black spot Hot-Shot

#50 metallic blue Hot-Shot

F-4 orange Flatfish

Trolling plugs

Keel sinkers are designed for trolling with unweighted thin-bladed spoons, unweighted spinners or gang trolls.

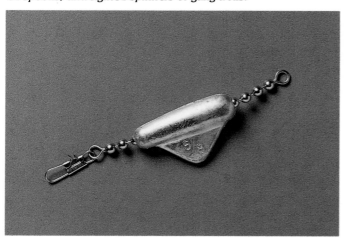

encounter. Again, experimentation is the key.

Be sure that your plug of choice runs "true." Most brands of trolling plugs track perfectly out of the package, that is they stay facing downward in a tight wobble with zero tendency to run right or left. If the plug runs predominantly to the left, right or flips over it needs to be tuned. Slightly turning the eye screw or bending the clip on the lip in the opposite direction will straighten it out. For example, if the plug wants to run right, turn the eye or bend the clip slightly to the left. Test plugs along side the boat at optimum trolling speed to be sure they run straight and true.

Trolling Bait

From time to time situations occur where standard trolling fare such as plugs, spoons and spinners won't attract trout. Unnatural as it may seem, trolling bait like nightcrawlers, minnows or maggots can be the answer.

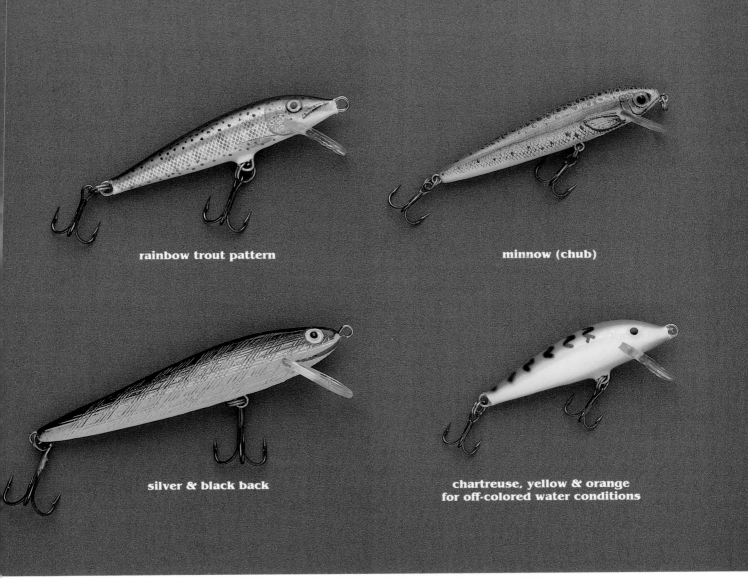

rainbow trout pattern

minnow (chub)

silver & black back

chartreuse, yellow & orange
for off-colored water conditions

Rapala diving plugs that resemble baitfish

Trolled bait are fished in tandem with an attractor, most commonly gang spinners, or "gang trolls" as they are called. Most spinner blade trolls consist of a plastic rudder and four to six spinner blades fixed on a flexible wire. At the end of the wire a 6 inch "snubber" is attached. A snubber is a section of rubber tubing that absorbs the shock from a strike, therefore protecting light leaders and lines. From a swivel at the end of the snubber a 10 to 24 inch section of 6 to 10 pound monofilament leader is tied. At the end of the leader a size 10, 8 or 6 bait hook is tied on. Add the bait of your choice and you are ready to troll.

Gang trolls in tandem with bait seem to be most effective in deeper or limited visibility water where more flash and smell is necessary to attract trout. Trolls appeal to several trout instincts and give off visual and underwater vibrations. Remember, multi-bladed gang trolls resist water when trolled, so you must use a heavier rod and mainline.

Gang troll rigging.

When trolling, stillfishing or drifting bait, adding a quality swivel to your terminal outfit helps prevent line-damaging twist.

Kokanee (landlocked sockeye salmon) are extremely choosy in what they strike. Trolling bait, primarily maggots, is sometimes the only way to catch them. Gang trolls are not necessary for kokanee, however. Unweighted "Wedding Ring" style spinners, characterized by a single small No. 0 or No. 1 silver-plated blade followed by a body consisting of 8 to 12 small red plastic beads separated by a tiny, round jeweled "ring" in the center of the spinner body, are standard for kokanee. At the end of the Wedding Ring spinner is a single bait hook, either size 8 or 10. From this hook hang 3 to 6 maggots. Attach the spinner/maggot combo 3 to 4 feet behind a bead chain style keel sinker or run off a downrigger 30 to 50 feet behind the boat. If fishing without the aid of downriggers, weight spinners accordingly to achieve proper depth.

"Trolling" from Shore

Many trout fishermen have no access to boats or fish waters that have restrictions on floating devices. The trouter confined to shore can employ the same trolling lures—usually spinners and spoons—and hook fish. One of the best shore casting lures is the Kastmaster which is basically a straight piece of metal with superior aerodynamic qualities allowing for longer casts. If you read water correctly you can find productive areas well within casting range of shore.

By using the "fan" casting method you can cover a large area of water in little time. Fan casting is exactly as it sounds. Standing in one spot and make a progressive series of casts (in the shape of a hand-held Oriental fan) from one side to the other. You may want to make the first fan pattern in close, then repeat the pattern by casting a few feet farther out.

Lake Stillfishing

"Stillfishing" lakes is exactly as it sounds; your presentation is made from a stationary position. Unlike trolling, a boat is not necessary and you substitute bait for lures. Stillfishing with bait has a reputation of being the "lazy" way to catch trout. However, positioning bait over trout feeding areas—where legal—is every bit as effective as trolling and often works better.

Where to begin stillfishing is determined in the same fashion as trolling. If the lake is a popular one simply look for a congregation of boats or bank anglers. Chances are excellent they are on or very near concentrations of trout. If other anglers are not present success depends on your water reading skills. Once you have determined proper

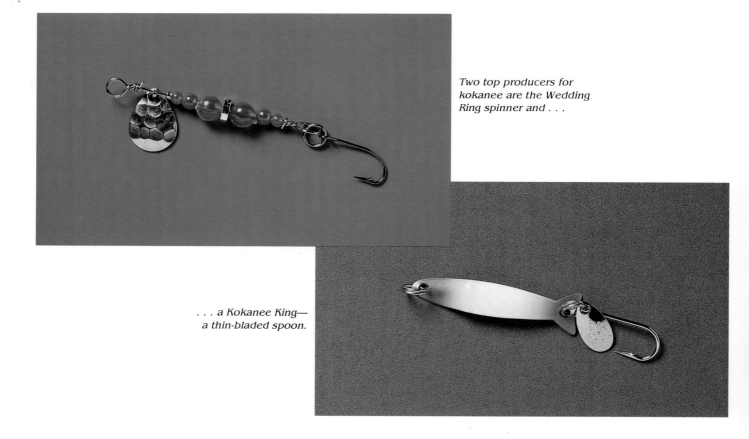

Two top producers for kokanee are the Wedding Ring spinner and . . .

. . . a Kokanee King— a thin-bladed spoon.

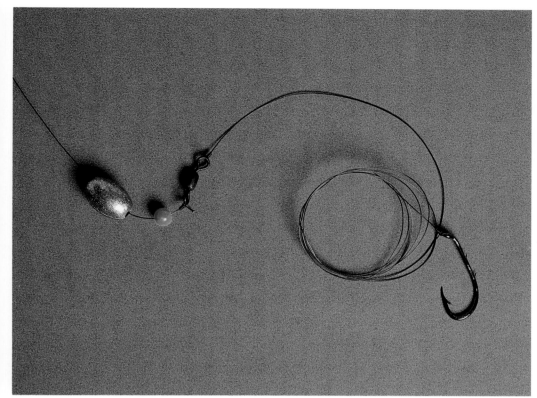

Lake stillfishing terminal rigging.

large trout use an 8 pound mainline with 3 to 4 feet of 6 pound leader.

How much weight is needed for stillfishing? Because lakes are practically current free, the absolute minimum amount of lead is all that is necessary. One to two small split shot gently squeezed onto the line (so you don't "bruise" the light monofilament) just above the swivel should sink any bait adequately. You want just enough weight to sink the bait to trout level, not so much that a fish can detect unnatural weight after it mouths the bait. In many situations, swivel weight alone sinks bait quite well. The smallest black—not chrome—swivels in sizes 10 and 12 are ideal for stillfishing.

When stillfishing from shore you obviously need more weight than when fishing out of a boat for casting and positioning purposes. Let's assume first that you are targeting trout on or near the bottom. In this case hollow core, egg-shaped sliding style sinkers are the choice for bank stillfishermen. These weights position bait nicely and by allowing mainlines to slip freely trout cannot feel any unnatural resistance. Non-sliding weights attached on mainlines cause trout to swiftly drop bait after weight is felt. Remember to leave a bit of slack in the mainline so trout can swim with the bait. This ensures you enough time to grab the rod and set a hook.

When stillfishing add just enough split shot to sink the bait.

depth and location where trout feed from studying temperature, structure, lighting and food sources half the battle is won. The other half is determining which bait to use and how to present it.

Stillfishing calls for light mainlines and leaders. When trolling trout zero in on lures and pay little heed to line. For this reason you can use heavier pound tests while trolling. Not so when stillfishing. Trout have all the time on earth to scrutinize your bait. Any hint of line attached to bait makes for an unnatural presentation and will be refused. Mainlines for stillfishing test from 4, 6 or 8 pounds and leaders 2, 4 or 6 pounds. Mainlines should be slightly heavier in case snags are encountered or, heaven forbid, a leviathan trout grabs your bait and heads for the horizon. In this case only the short section of leader is broken off and needs to be replaced.

When stillfishing ultra clear water or targeting pan-size trout, 4 pound mainlines and 2 pound leaders are a good match. Leaders should be a minimum of 3 feet and a maximum of 5 feet long to visually separate bait from weights and swivels. (More on these shortly.) The smallest hooks are used with this combination due to wary fish in clear water and more importantly, force transfer. Two pound test cannot take much shock from a hookset. Therefore, smaller hooks are necessary as tinier, finer points are more easily set into the bony mouth of a trout.

When fishing deeper clear water in low light or for slightly larger trout (14 inches to several pounds), use 6 pound mainline and 4 pound leader. Leaders should be 2-1/2 to 4 feet long. This setup is ideal for all-around stillfishing and is a good choice to start with when fishing unfamiliar lakes. When fishing cloudy water, or targeting

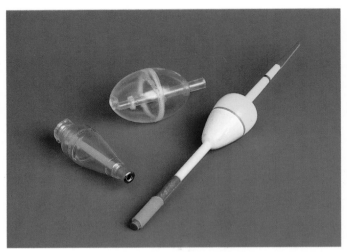

Floats add an extra dimension for the shore-bound trout angler by allowing you to position baits near surface-feeding fish, add weight for increased casting distance and keep baits in perfect position while drifting downstream.

If trout are cruising near or on the surface, a float or "bobber" is the choice. By simply fixing the float 3 to 4 feet above your bait you can present the offering near the surface. There are many styles of floats, but the rule to remember is the smaller the float, the better the result. The easier a trout can pull one under, the less chance that it will spit out the bait before you can set the hook. The float's weight along with the bait is normally plenty of weight to propel casts from shore.

A floating bait used by itself or in tandem with your chosen bait is a necessity when bottom fishing from shore. Because most productive areas in lakes are near weedbeds. Bait resting inside weeds and lying on the bottom cannot be found easily by trout. Mini-marshmallows or floating dough-type bait such as Berkley Power Bait, Atlas' Mr. Trout Glo Pellets or Zeke's Floatin' Bait slid onto the hook and placed above the hook eye hold bait above weeds, making easy targets for cruising fish.

Floating baits position your offering above weeds and into a cruising trout's cone of vision.

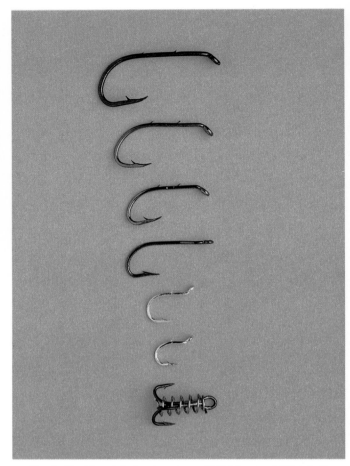

Use baitholder-style hooks when stillfishing or drifting bait.

Hooks for stillfishing need to match your bait to present it naturally and hidden from a trout's view. Even though hook manufacturers make hooks in various colors, it matters little when hooks are buried inside bait. For this reason, unless you firmly believe a specific color of hook increases hookup ratios, standard bronze finishes are adequate. Each bait has hooks that compliment it.

Tiny delicate bait such as caddis larvae, mayfly nymphs, scuds or maggots, cannot hold together if a thick hook is forced through their fragile bodies. Fine wire hooks in size 14 (smallest), 12 and 10 (largest) are good choices for these baits. Salmon eggs require fully rounded hooks that hide completely inside single eggs. Single salmon eggs are best matched with size 8 or 10 egg-style hook. Larger or more formidable bait such as worms, nightcrawlers, hellgrammites, leeches, crayfish, sculpin or minnows accept a regular heavier bronze baitholder-style hook. Baitholder-style hooks have down-turned eyes and commonly two tiny barbs on the shank. Common sizes are 4 (largest, for minnows and sculpins), 6, 8, 10 and 12. For dough-type bait like Power Bait or cheese you may want to try tiny treble hooks to help hold bait tightly onto hooks. Trebles in sizes 10 and 12 work well and there are trebles available with coiled springs around the shanks to help keep moldable bait in place.

Look for quality names when buying hooks, cheaper hooks will not hold a point and can break, even on small

Single salmon eggs are easy to obtain and one of the best trout baits for lakes and streams.

"Stripping" For Kokanee

Kokanee as a rule do not take the same lures and bait as trout. Besides the occasional kernel of white corn, there is one specific bait, terminal rigging and stillfishing technique that consistently takes kokanee. The method is called stripping.

Kokanee have a fondness for maggots and the color red. The terminal rig consists of a size 10 or 12 hook with red thread wrapped around the shank. On the curved base of the hook place 4 to 6 maggots hooked just under the tough skin of their "heads." Use a 4 pound mainline and 3-1/2 to 4 feet of 3 pound test leader.

Attach one small split shot—just enough to reach bottom—and bring the maggot/red fly rig toward the surface in short, 3 to 6 inch "strips" either by pulling line in with your free hand or by reeling. The correct rhythm is a slow strip, pause, strip, pause. My uncle was an expert stripper for kokanee. His words of wisdom were, "If you think you are stripping in too slow, go slower." Kokanee are extremely light biters and will hang onto this rig for only a split-second. When the rod tip hesitates, strike immediately.

trout! Names like Gamakatsu, Eagle Claw, VMC, Mustad and Tru-Turn are trusted and proven.

When stillfishing from a boat you don't have to be anchored to present a bait. Drifting along with a slight breeze allows you to cover more water and present your bait over a wider area.

Rivers and Creeks: Presenting Lures and Bait

Flowing waters such as rivers and creeks offer a bitter-sweet challenge. Unlike lakes, streams have much less area

These tiny #12 Mack's Glo Hooks are ideal for stripping for kokanee. Just add maggots to the bend of the hook.

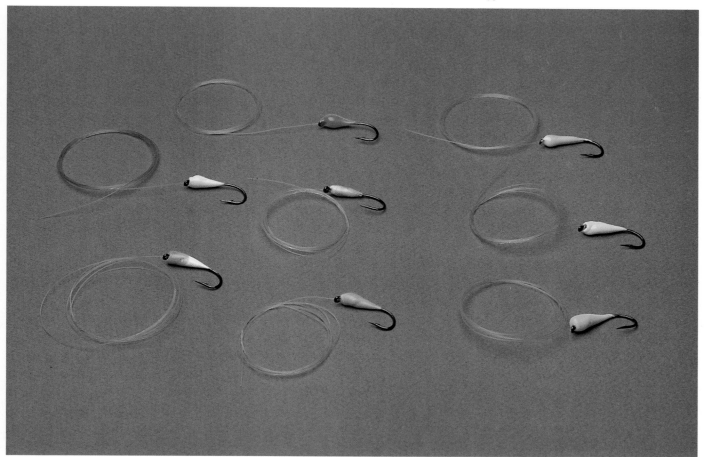

for trout to hide and once we learn how to read flowing water, finding them is much easier. However, ever changing currents, depth, flow and bottom structure more than make up the degree of difficulty.

Positioning

Before discussing lures and bait we have to address positioning; where to start a presentation on a section of holding water. First, we'll look at positioning on rivers and large streams. The first rule of proper positioning is to always start at the uppermost section of holding water. It doesn't matter if you are standing above or below this spot, as access, current speed or lure selection can sometimes dictate, make initial casts above the area where you expect the first trout to be holding under current conditions.

There are two reasons for starting at the top of the holding water. First, and most important, is that it allows the lure or bait to be presented in front of any or all trout. A trout's greatest range of vision is directly above and in front. When the offering is placed above, trout can see it easier and faster. Second, there is less chance your mainline or lure will accidently bump a fish from its blind side frightening it. Bumped fish are results of random casting.

Once you have determined where to begin working the upper portion of holding water you must now gauge a workable casting distance. You want to work the shortest amount of line and still be able to adequately cover the water. Have no more line out than you can readily control. Less line out means more control over presentations and greater hooksetting force. Shorter lines reduce line drag which result in slack. Slack causes speeded-up presentations, even faster than present water flows. Trout will not accept a lure or pick up a bait if it is travelling faster than the current. Fishing a short line means less line stretch. Less stretch means less feel is lost—important with fast-striking or soft mouthing trout. You can get closer to trout in broken water than in flat, calm stretches.

The Standard Swing Presentation

After you have determined a proper starting position at the top end of the holding water, present your bait or lure. The standard swing presentation is precisely as it sounds; it can be used for almost 90 percent of all river situations when trout fishing.

The idea of the standard swing is to allow terminal gear to be presented in front of the first trout in the run. Casting angle is determined by water depth and speed. For example, if the holding water in front of you is shallow or slow, it requires a cast below your position. If the water is swift or deep, your cast must be placed above your position to allow it sufficient time to sink to trout eye level. If your casts are landing too far up or downstream for you to be in immediate control of line, lure or bait, you have to change angles to achieve a comfortable working distance.

After you have made the proper adjustments of angle, or perhaps choice of lure, you can start to work the water. The swing presentation is casting inside a framework, often referred to as casting in a grid or fan casting. Start with the shortest possible cast, gradually increasing distance with each cast working outward. You will be working out and then down from your original starting position. Your presentations will travel and "swing" downward from your position, at or slightly slower than current speed. Numbers of casts made in one area vary by size of the holding water and water visibility. For example, if there is 4 feet of visibility, then casts are made 4 feet out and 4 feet apart.

When your presentation is swinging around while traveling downstream, how natural the drift looks depends solely on rod angle and body positioning. When fishing in rivers

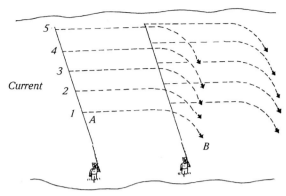

Starting at the top of the holding water, the angler begins working the drift by casting to spot "A" and allowing the terminal gear to travel along with the current until swinging toward shore. (B) The angler will gradually lengthen his casts (1 thru 5) to cover the section of holding water. The number of casts in one position will vary, depending on the size of the holding water and degrees of visibility. For example, two feet of visibility, two feet between casts, etc. When all water has been worked in one position, step downstream to a new position and resume casting, how far to step again depends on visibility—two feet of visibility, step two feet downstream. Casting area is overlapped so no fish will be missed or spooked. Repeat until all holding water is worked.

and large streams mainline and terminal gear is pulled against the current force of the flow pushing gear and line up toward the surface, out of the trout's range of vision. It then becomes the angler's duty to use rod angle and body positioning to negate the push of water.

How high do you hold your rod when making the swing presentation? As each cast is made longer to cover the water you must hold the rod higher to keep the mainline from catching in the current. Doing this prevents line belly, which is the primary reason for an unnatural presentation. Keep in mind, however, the higher the rod is held, the less "back-strike" area is left to set a hook. Ideal rod angle is between 9 o'clock, which is straight out, to 11 o'clock. A relaxed 10 o'clock position is best for river and large stream fishing.

River Lures

There are just two basic lures for rivers and large streams: spinners and spoons. Spinners have the greatest versatility as they can be fished from any angle. Quality spinners with immediate, responsive blade spins work effectively from downstream of your target water as well as upstream because they are the only style of lure that works when pulled with the current. Spinner sizes and colors for rivers range from No. 0 to No. 4, depending on water speed, depth, temperature and clarity. With this many combinations of variables, you would need over 100 different spinners to match conditions year-round. In early morning, evening, dark cloudy days, colder water temperatures (45 degrees or lower) or limited visibility water, use larger spinners from No. 3 to No. 4 with bright blades in silver plate and bright colored bodies. For normal overcast days, shaded areas, medium water temperatures (45 to 60 degrees) and clear water use popular sized trout spinners in sizes No. 1 to No. 3 with brass blades and natural toned bodies. For bright sun, clear water, warmer water temperatures (58 to 70 degrees) or spooky, heavily pressured fish, go as small as possible with No. 0 or No. 1 dull brass or black blades with olive, brown or black bodies.

As the line becomes tight after casting, your bait or lure will start to rise. Now you have to turn yourself downstream and follow the drift down with the rod. There will again be a point, even after you have turned and dipped your arm toward you terminal gear, where the line tightens and begins to rise again. If there is more water to work you have to give a bit of line from the reel to stay in contact or proximity of bottom. If the piece of holding water is short be prepared to reel in line to keep lures and bait out of tackle-eating rocks. Experience is again the key to knowing which to do when.

Spoons for rivers should always be the weighted casting type. Spoons of this type perform their best with no added weight; lead placed on the mainline dulls sensations of the working lure to your rod. Spoons should always be cast below your position, because they need current to impart proper action. Unlike spinners they need considerable current pushing on them to work at their optimum. As when

Four of the better designs of lures for river use: the Rooster Tail weighted spinner . . .

. . . the Blue Fox Vibrax . . .

. . . the teardrop-shaped Stee-Lee spoon . . .

. . . and the elongated Krokodile Spoon.

trolling, spoons give off more trout attracting flash when they wobble. When spoons start to spin they become buoyant and cannot be fished deeply. Remember: fat spoons sink much slower and work higher than narrow spoons because of a higher surface area to weight ratio.

As with spinners, spoon weights and colors depend on current speed, depth, temperature and clarity. Spoons from 1/8, 1/4 and 1/2 ounce cover almost all types of trout holding water, with 1/3 and 2/5 ounce spoons used in rare deep water presentations. In cold water (33 to 42 degrees), limited visibility, early morning and evening, silver plate has greater reflection. For overcast days, medium water temperatures (45 to 60 degrees) and clear water, try to match spoon color with baitfish in the system. Larger predatory trout key on natural colors more than any metal finish, however, brass or copper sometimes work well. Even in warmer water temperatures and bright sunny days, stay with natural fish colors for spoons.

Drifting Bait

Whereas you may fish spinners and spoons at slightly slower speeds cross-current to impart action and still receive strikes, your cast to strike ratio will not be as high unless baits are fished exactly or as close as possible to existing current speed. That is the key to drifting bait.

Terminal rigs for drifting bait closely resemble those used for stillfishing. The matching of mainline and leader are the same: 4 pound mainline with 2 pound leader for smaller trout, clear water or skittish, heavily pressured fish; 6 pound mainline with 4 pound leader for average sized trout or as a basic setup for new and unfamiliar waters; and 8 pound mainline with 6 pound leader for large trout or limited water visibility.

However, leaders should be a bit shorter than those used for stillfishing. Trout that live in flowing water cannot afford to be too picky when a morsel comes drifting by. They often have only a split second to decide to take or refuse. In this

bottom that prohibits a drift due to its tackle-eating nature, a float allows you to work these types of water with ease. In water that may be too slow for even an unweighted bait, a float keeps bait moving along with even the slowest current. If a section of holding water is beyond your casting distance downriver, simply feeding line to the float will carry bait down with the current as far as you can control your line. If the bottom has large boulders, tree branches or any of the like that instantly snags terminal gear, you may suspend bait just above the terminal eaters. For bait, trout will come farther than you may think.

A simple all-around rigging for floats is to affix your terminal gear on the float so it suspends bait at an approximate depth of one to 2 feet above bottom. Add one small split shot one foot above the bait to keep it down. Floats not only present bait at exact current speeds, they allow you to fish a grid from any angle without fear of snagging bottom.

Small Creeks

For small streams and creeks, presentation is dictated by any angle of approach that does not spook trout. Due to the nature of tiny stream fishing, you will be working small pockets, undercuts, etc., places that require only a cast or two to properly work the section of holding water.

Lures for small streams and creeks are limited to tiny spinners in sizes No. 0 and No. 1, due to the spinner's ability to work at any direction from any angle. Tiny marabou jigs in 1/64 and 1/32 ounce are also perfect for small streams. Perhaps nothing works as well in this diminutive water as bait. Lines should test the same as they do on larger waters, but leaders will be 8 to 12 inches long. You must get bait down immediately in these cramped quarters; longer leaders do not sink bait fast enough to reach a trout's window of vision.

The Fly and Bubble

As all fly fishermen know, during an aquatic insect hatch there is no better technique than to present an imitation of the same. During hatches, it is common for trout to ignore even the best presented lures or bait and focus their attention strictly on insects. When you are spin fishing a lake or stream, it is possible to use artificial flies with your outfit. What it requires is the addition of a clear casting bubble.

First, before rigging the fly and bubble, you have to "match the hatch." This means you must choose a fly that closely resembles the size and color of the insect and present it in a manner that approximates its' movements. Trout can be very selective, even during a hatch. A fly that is too large, is the wrong color or moves unnaturally will be ignored.

The best type of spinning bubble for use with flies is the

case separation of bait from weights and swivels is not as critical for success. Leaders from 2 to 2-1/2 feet are plenty long and can be as short as one foot when water visibility is low or when fishing very fast water.

For weight simply crimp on enough split shot to sink bait but not so much to make terminal gear come in frequent contact with the bottom. Remember, trout can only look up and in front of them, so a bait drifted in close proximity of bottom will get their attention. Terminal gear that is over-weighted has a 100 percent greater chance of snagging than with very little weight and will not drift naturally. Instead of crimping shot directly onto mainline as you would for stillfishing, leave a 4 inch tag end of line off the swivel when tying on a leader. Lightly squeeze split shot onto the tag end, creating a dropper of lead. If the split shot works its way between rocks, a pull will free your terminal gear. Some bait, like nightcrawlers, leeches or small crayfish, are heavy enough on their own to sink and drift quite nicely without added weight.

Some bait, such as grasshoppers and crickets, should be fished with no added weight for a natural presentation. By employing a fine wire hook and feeding line to create zero drag, these bait can be fished on top where trout expect them.

Floats can open up a river to bait fishermen. In water that may be too slow to achieve a drift, or if a section of water is beyond reasonable casting distance or even has a clear, oval bubble that is tapered on one end. Clear bubbles are not as easily seen by trout. These will either have tiny clips at each end for holding the line or have a rubber band through the center. The rubber band style is probably the best, as they are less abrasive on lines. To attach these style bubbles, feed the mainline through he center and put enough twists into the rubber band until it no longer can slide freely. Both of these styles allow you to adjust the length of line between bubble and fly without retying. Attach the bubble on the mainline with the wider end facing the fly. With the tapered end facing you, there is little water resistance when retrieving or working the fly.

An ideal setup for the fly and bubble is a 6 pound mainline joining a 4 pound leader. Tie the leader on to the mainline with a tiny #12 black swivel or blood knot. Separation length between the fly and the casting bubble should be no less than 3 feet. This is important for two reasons. First, you do not want the trout to see the bubble, and second the minimum 3 foot length allows the fly a more natural float, either on a lake surface or along with stream currents. A maximum length of 5 feet is suggested because any longer of a separation between the fly and bubble makes it difficult to cast and will cost you accuracy and distance.

The fly and bubble is not restricted for use with only dry flies during hatches. Nymphs can be fished as effectively in lakes and streams by adding a tiny split shot on to the leader approximately 1-1/2 to 2 feet above the fly. When fishing nymphs, after the cast lands in the water allow a bit of time for the splash rings to dissipate before giving any motion to the fly. This gives trout time to settle down. The same is true for dries, allow a few seconds before beginning the retrieve.

Casting bubbles with flies allows you to cover greater distances and more water faster than is possible with a fly rod. It will pay off for you to learn insect hatches on your favorite trout water and carry a fly and bubble outfit to match them. The outfit not only saves you from fishless days, but also may work so well it may turn out to be your chosen technique.

How to Release Trout

Play and release trout as rapidly as your gear allows. Stand in a spot that is out of stronger currents when playing fish. Trout tire more quickly when they cannot use the current to their advantage.

After landing a trout keep it in the water as much as possible. Grasping the fish will remove much of its protective slime coat and may cause internal damage. If you want a quick photo, gently cradle the fish on its belly immediately behind the pectoral fins and firmly, without squeezing, grasp the wrist of the tail.

Remove the hook(s) as gently and rapidly as possible with needle-nosed pliers or hemostats. If the trout is deeply hooked, cut the leader and leave the hook in the fish. Natural body acids will eventually dissolve the hook.

Hold the trout upright in slower flowing current facing upstream. Allow the trout time to recover. When the fish has regained its equilibrium it will start to struggle and show renewed strength. Let go of the tail and let it swim off to be caught another day.

Knots

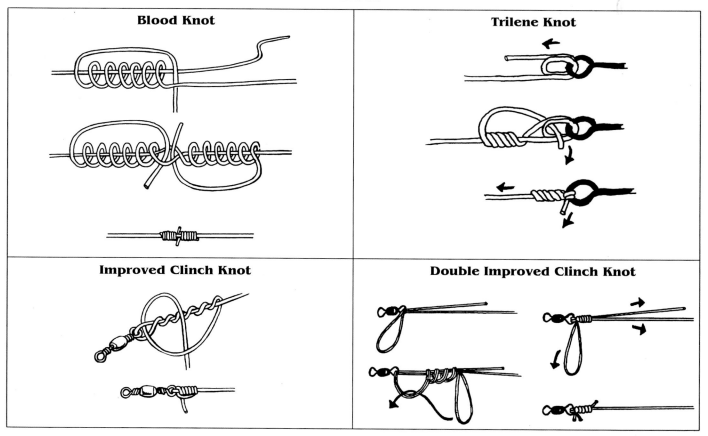

LEARN MORE ABOUT FLY FISHING AND FLY TYING WITH THESE BOOKS

If you are unable to find the books shown below at your local book store
or fly shop you can order direct from the publisher below.

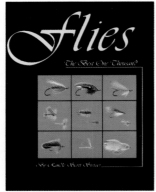

Flies: The Best One Thousand
Randy Stetzer
$24.95

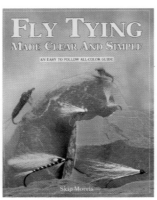

Fly Tying Made Clear and Simple
Skip Morris
$19.95 (HB: $29.95)

The Art of Tying the Dry Fly
Skip Morris
$29.95(HB:$39.95)

Curtis Creek Manifesto
Sheridan Anderson
$7.95

American Fly Tying Manual
Dave Hughes
$9.95

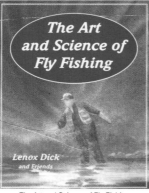

The Art and Science of Fly Fishing
Lenox Dick
$19.95

Western Hatches
Dave Hughes, Rick Hafele
$24.95

Lake Fishing with a Fly
Ron Cordes, Randall Kaufmann
$26.95

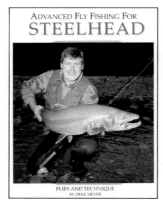

Advanced Fly Fishing for Steelhead
Deke Meyer
$24.95

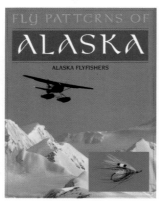

Fly Patterns of Alaska
Alaska Flyfishers
$19.95

Fly Tying & Fishing for Panfish and Bass
Tom Keith
$19.95

Float Tube Fly Fishing
Deke Meyer
$11.95

VISA, MASTERCARD or AMERICAN EXPRESS ORDERS CALL TOLL FREE: 1-800-541-9498
(9-5 Pacific Standard Time)

Or Send Check or money order to:

Frank Amato Publications
Box 82112
Portland, Oregon 97282

(Please add $3.00 for shipping and handling)